This May Be Difficult to Read

But You **Really** Should
(for your child's sake)

This book is dedicated to my favorite reading buddies:
Josh, Sasha, Finn & Russ

In loving memory of Papa Bear.
Marvin, you have a special place in my heart
and you are always in my thoughts.

Literacy is a bridge from misery to hope.

It is a tool for daily life in modern society.

It is a bulwark against poverty, and a building block of development, an essential complement to investments in roads, dams, clinics and factories. Literacy is a platform for democratization, and a vehicle for the promotion of cultural and national identity.

Especially for girls and women, it is an agent of family health and nutrition.

For everyone, everywhere, literacy is, along with education in general, a basic human right . . .

Literacy is, finally, the road to human progress and the means through which every man, woman and child can realize his or her full potential.

–Kofi Annan, 1997

CONTENTS

ABOUT THE AUTHOR
OR WHO DO I THINK I AM?

Given that this is a book about you and your children, you might be wondering, who do I think I am and why should you listen to a word that I say?

Well, I'm a cognitive developmental psychologist. I've taught in the classroom for over 30 years and I've raised 3 of my own children! I've seen the struggle firsthand.

I've watched my children (and possibly your children) succeed and fail with phonics, reading, reading comprehension, and learning. I've seen our collective children hurting and I've also seen them succeed beyond their wildest dreams. I have such a passion for watching them develop a love for reading and learning that I wanted to share it with you.

I earned my PhD from Stony Brook University in 1994 and I have been teaching and raising children ever since. I have marveled at the educational successes and failures of my own 3 children (the last of whom is now off to university).

I have also been teaching at my local community college for over 20 years, and while I have seen many of my students succeed, I have also watched some of them struggle badly with the printed word. These are clearly highly verbal students, but their reading comprehension skills sell them short in the classroom. Granted, textbooks aren't easy to read—they are often packed full of facts that develop concepts at a staggering pace—but how were these students prepared for college-level reading? What was their early childhood experience? Will your child be one of the success stories or will your child struggle with textbooks and comprehending the printed word?

This book is about success! This book is about inspiring the greatest number of children to love reading and the comprehension process so that they can't wait to pick up a book or dive into a textbook (that might be a tad too optimistic, but you get the point).

Aside from my work in the classroom, I have given lectures around the country, published magazine articles, served as an "Ask the Expert" for *Texas Family Magazine*, edited books for McGraw Hill, worked as a consultant for Relay/GSE, and presented workshops and lectures for the "Distinguished Speaker Series" and the Child Care Councils of Suffolk and Nassau County, New York.

My publications, lectures, and workshops cover such topics as:

- "The 21st Century Brain and Other Stories"
- "Pixels vs. Play: A Cognitive Developmental Exploration of Play"
- "Neuropsychology and Cognition in the Classroom"
- "Reading: The Magic Formula"
- "Stop Playing and Learn Something"
- "What's Next, Calculus in Kindergarten?"
- "Reading It All Wrong"

- "Learning to Read and Reading to Learn"
- "The Impact of Technology on Cognitive Growth"
- "What Do We Tell the Parents? Explaining Developmentally Appropriate Practices in the Classroom"
- "Unlocking the Mysteries of Play: A Cognitive Developmental Perspective"
- "A B Seeing: The Challenges of Reading through the Eyes of a Child"

So, who do I think I am? I hope that I am a catalyst that will inspire change in our homes and in our classrooms so that children of all ages and backgrounds will fall in love with reading and learn to use the printed word to think, grow, and challenge the status quo.

How will I accomplish this, you ask? Well, it is my deepest hope that this book will help you to think as a child thinks. This book, which highlights 60 years of cognitive developmental research (and lighter anecdotal evidence!), is based on this research. I hope that this insight will alleviate some of the frustration that we often experience when we try to teach our children. Together we can look at the learning process through a child's eyes and more fully appreciate how children think, learn, and process information within the context of learning to read and comprehend the written word.

Remember, their brains are different from our brains. They don't think, speak, or learn like we do. Let's learn from their perspective so we can appreciate why "this may be difficult to read" . . .

INTRODUCTION

FACT OR MYTH

A s adults, it is often difficult for us to remember how we actually learned certain skills, such as walking, talking, or reading. It seems so automatic to us now (we call this automaticity[2]). This automaticity can cause us to forget the sometimes agonizing steps that are involved in each process, such as reading comprehension (see Chapter 5 for more details). In addition, the "hindsight bias"[3] can leave us with a set of mistaken beliefs, such as:

Reading is easy—just look at the words,

or

If you see letters → say the letters → then you'll understand what is written . . .

This, in turn, can lead to many mistaken myths about children and early literacy.

Take the test below and see if you can separate fact from fiction regarding early literacy and learning.

Fact or myth (circle the facts):

- If children can "sound out" the words, then children can "read."

- "Earlier is better" when it comes to learning to read.

- Listening to classical music will make your child smarter.

- Smaller words are easier to read.

- It's "cheating" to tell your child the words that he or she gets "stuck" on.

- If your child can repeat a sentence out loud then he or she understands its meaning.

- Telling children facts will make them smarter.

- It is cheating to look at the pictures to figure out what the words say or mean.

- Early Childhood programs that focus on learning the ABCs and reading are more educational than programs that focus on play.

- It is better for your child to read to you than for you to read to your child.

Turn the page for the
correct answers . . .

Read on to find out why each of these statements is actually false—they are all myths!

The following chapters will provide insight, derived from 60 years of cognitive developmental psychology, that debunks these 10 myths about reading and early childhood education.

CHAPTER 1

READICULOUS

Over 42,000,000 American adults are defined as functionally illiterate, which means that they can't follow the directions on a can of soup.[4] That's readiculous. They can read the words out loud, but they can't comprehend or utilize their meaning. If they all went to school and if they were all taught to read, then what went wrong?

Within our schools, our children are failing to comprehend at staggeringly high rates. Fewer than 33% of eighth-grade students achieved grade-level proficiency in recent state exams.[5] That means that 67% of these eighth graders can't read proficiently. Why is this happening? What specifically is it that they can't do in such enormous numbers by eighth grade and what, exactly, are we doing about it?

Although our eighth graders are collectively falling behind, the story isn't so grim across all the other grades. It appears that the test results in the lower grades aren't as awful. In fourth grade, for example, approximately 60% of our students achieved grade-level proficiency in English. What, then, is happening to our children between fourth and eighth grade? Do their reading skills deteriorate? Do the test demands become exponentially harder as they move through middle school? How do we account for these diabolical declines in literacy? Do we teach our children to read and then they, subsequently, forget everything we taught them? Or are we, perhaps, teaching our children incorrectly?

We are a society that is obsessed with teaching children to read at an increasingly younger age. Many conscientious parents are fixated on teaching their preschoolers to read. Many working parents expect their child care providers and preschool teachers to assume this task on their behalf. There is a prevailing sense in our community that literacy should be achieved even before their child sets foot in a kindergarten classroom. Yet, regardless of this early tuition, many of these children fail at staggeringly high rates as they progress through our educational system. Why is that?

Pinpointing the reasons for this decline offers us a bastion of hope that we can resolve this reading conundrum. The answers lie deeply embedded within 60 years of research in cognitive developmental psychology that is the cornerstone of our understanding of the reading process. Let's take a good look at the reading process and assess what's actually involved in successful reading. Together we can tease apart what we're currently teaching our children about reading, what we fail to teach them, and what we could be doing differently to improve our children's literacy.

If you looked back in time to see how reading has been taught over the years, you may initially be inclined to believe that there's been very little evolution. The teaching of reading doesn't appear to have changed much since Dick and Jane, or Adam and Eve, for that matter, learned to read. You may indeed, be correct!

Today's reading issues are not new; we have known for the last 20 years that our children's reading comprehension skills are below par; in fact, way below par.[6] We have a slew of research that shows that children can't read[7]: We have test after standardized test scores confirming that our children can't read. We have affirmations of this annually, at each grade level. To confirm our worst fears about our nation's comprehension incompetence, we offer remedial reading at the college level and our students flock to it. The statistics are staggering.

- 70% of high school students end up needing some kind of remedial reading class[8]
- In the last 15 years, 15 million students have graduated from our high schools reading below the basic reading level[9]
- 1 in 5 college students enroll in remedial reading classes in their freshman year of college[10]
- Remediation has cost families nearly $1.5 billion[11]
- 45% of these students are in middle- and upper-income homes[12]

At this point in our lives, we competent readers read so effortlessly that we tend to take each step in the process for granted. This makes it increasingly more difficult for us to fully appreciate the challenges reading presents to the novice reader, confounding our ability to teach them effectively or offer any helpful, strategic advice.

As you read through these chapters, you will be able to shift your perspective so that you can experience reading through the eyes of a child, replete with all of their limitations and inadequacies. Together we can analyze why, as a society, we seem to be failing to educate our nation's children and why so many parents obsess so unsuccessfully over this process. We can hypothesize about why we marvel at early readers and why we worry compulsively about our slower learners. Together we can begin a new dialogue with our nation's parents to reinvent our approach to reading comprehension in early childhood education.

Together, we can change our approach toward the teaching of reading. We can reinvent reading instruction to turn the challenge of reading into an exhilarating journey.

CHAPTER 2

GOAL: READING BEFORE KINDERGARTEN

MYTH:
"Your baby can read"
or "Earlier is better"

Let's start at the beginning—kindergarten . . .

Many parents decide that they'd like their preschooler or toddler to be a reader before the bell even rings on the first day of kindergarten. They seek out a child care center or preschool program that will satisfy this educational goal. Across the country, we parents are painstakingly teaching children letters and their corresponding sounds. We use drills and practice until our children develop fluency, and presto, we have ourselves a reader! While it is entirely possible for 5, 4 and even 3-year olds to read aloud, from a cognitive perspective, it is not the greatest idea. Here are the top 10 reasons why you shouldn't teach your child to read aloud before kindergarten (which I discuss in more detail in future chapters):

The Top 10 Reasons Why You Shouldn't Teach Your Child to Read Aloud before Kindergarten

1. THE HIPPOCAMPUS: Our brain has to be mature enough to benefit from reading instruction. The brain takes time to grow and develop; the hippocampus, for example, is involved in the retention of long-term memories, which are an essential component in the reading process. It takes time for the brain to mature or "myelinate."

2. MYELINATION: As we will discuss in future chapters, myelination is the process by which our neural pathways are coated with a fatty sheath that helps messages be sent more efficiently. During early childhood, that myelin sheath is still forming, so messages travel slower and experience more interruptions. As a result, there's a benefit to waiting until more of those neural pathways are myelinated before we begin formal education (see Chapter 3).

3. THE RETICULAR FORMATION: In order to read, we have to be old enough to concentrate and pay attention. This is not just a question of encouraging our children to sit still long enough to listen; the reticular formation within the brain has to develop so that our children can succeed at this task. This, once again, involves myelination, a biological process that cannot be rushed (again, see Chapter 3).

4. IMMATURE VISION: Children's eyes take time to mature, and it is often very difficult for them to tell the difference between a b→d or a q→p. To young children, they all look like balls and sticks (e.g. lo versus ol). When vision is more mature, it will be easier to differentiate between b and d or p and q.

5. PROPOSITION INTEGRATION: If we focus on reading aloud instead of reading for meaning, this could lead to problems later on in a child's educational journey, as they may find it hard to extract meaning from a text. Reading for meaning involves "proposition integration," a cognitively demanding task that may overwhelm our early childhood population. We will discuss how we take the information in a story and build ideas. As adults, we can read aloud and integrate propositions at the same time, but early readers use most of their cognitive capacity just trying to say the words out loud. Listen to how slowly they read and how much effort they put into each word.

6. SCHEMATIC KNOWLEDGE: Even if they can say the words out loud, at the tender age of 5, 4, or even 3, children often lack the real-world experience that is necessary to understand what they are reading. This "schematic" knowledge is essential for reading comprehension. As we will discuss, saying the words out loud, or "decoding," is an important part of the reading process, but we also have to apply meaning to those words, and that can take a level of experience that 3, 4, and even 5-year-olds often lack.

7. NURTURING A "LOVE FOR READING": Early readers don't always develop a love for reading. Asking a child at too young an age to "sound out words," and the drills and practice associated with doing so, can sometimes turn a child off to the whole reading process. We can nurture lifelong readers by keeping reading exciting, risk-free, and fun! When we read to our children, we can discuss what's happening at any given moment, who the characters remind us of, their possible motives, and we can also predict possible outcomes.

8. TOO MUCH PRESSURE: Children often love being read to, so focusing reading time on asking a child to say the words aloud can rob a child of that quality literary experience. Reading to your children so that they can learn to picture a story in their heads will establish reading as an exciting adventure. Reading a variety of texts, from poems and riddles to picture and chapter books, will increase this development.

9. WHAT THEY'LL MISS OUT ON: Think of all the wonderful, fun activities you are not engaging in when you are focused on drills and practice for reading fluency. Ironically, these are often the very activities that lay the foundation for educational success once the brain is mature and ready for formal instruction. Books are about life (albeit real or imaginary), so life experience is actually a key component of the reading process (see #6!).

10. CREATING A PASSION FOR READING: You only get one chance to teach your child the magic and majesty of reading, so why not do it in the best way possible? There are 60 years' worth of research by Piaget, Bransford, Pressley, Levin, Elkind, and other great scientists that clearly articulates how we can maximize each child's learning experience and reading comprehension competence. HINT: It isn't by focusing on decoding!

Bonus Reason!

EARLIER ISN'T BETTER: Earlier is just earlier! What will they do in kindergarten if they can read before they get there? Accelerating learning is not the same as increasing our breadth of knowledge. Educationally speaking, earlier is not always better. As we will see, decoding has to be equated with meaning for comprehension skills to develop successfully.

Just Forget It!

We, as a society, tend to fixate on this notion that earlier is better, but research suggests that we can't even recall information until our brain has reached a certain level of maturity.

Think back to the time when you were a newborn or an infant. What's the first thing that you remember? Truth be told, it is not likely that you remember anything before the age of 3 or 4, thanks to infant amnesia. Infantile amnesia, to use its proper term, credits this total breakdown in memory function to an immature hippocampus.[13] The hippocampus is the storage facility in the brain that holds and processes memories, but it's believed that it doesn't perform this process well for those first 3–4 years. The jury is still out on whether these memories aren't stored at all or whether they're just stored in an irretrievable format. Either way, amnesia is still the same end result; we recall nothing. If you fervently believe that you can recall the birth canal, your first bath, or any other potential firsts, then you may actually be experiencing what are called pseudo memories.[14] In other words, you may be confusing the stories your parents told you with reality or you may have heard the same stories repeatedly over the years until you can no longer differentiate between what you heard and what you actually experienced.

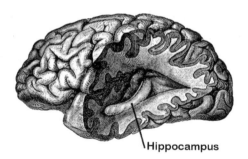

Hippocampus

15

MYTH:
"Your baby can read"
or "Earlier is better"

MYTH BUSTER:
Your baby can't read and earlier isn't better . . .

Now you can reasonably explain why earlier literacy is not "better." You know that the brain is not yet mature (because the hippocampus is still myelinating and the reticular formation is still developing). This makes remembering and sitting still somewhat challenging for our preschool population.

CHAPTER 3

BUT EVERYONE ELSE IS DOING IT . . . SAME SONG SECOND VERSE . . .

MYTH:
"Your baby can read" or "Earlier is better"

Hmm, that sounds familiar, doesn't it? I'm sure you may remember using this as a childhood excuse for almost anything: "But everyone else is doing it." Just because a large number of people is doing something, doesn't make it right. Yet we are often swayed by the preponderance of "evidence," albeit anecdotal, that "earlier is better." Tiger Woods, for example, started playing golf at 3 years of age; Mozart was a musical prodigy by age 5; and Bobby Fisher was a chess champion by 12. So why not give our children an early boost and maybe uncover their inner genius?

This type of thinking falls prey to the "confirmation bias,"[16] or our tendency to look for examples that confirm our expectations. In this case, these geniuses began at an early age, confirming our belief that starting early creates geniuses. This type of faulty logic fails to account for the millions of 3-, 5- and 12-year-olds who aren't golf experts, music prodigies, or chess champions at any point in their childhood, adolescence, or adulthood. In other words, prodigies can start at an early age, but starting early does not a prodigy make.

Human nature can, however, make us overprotective, and in our efforts to provide the best possible environment for our children, our thinking may become skewed. The "fallacy of positive instances" is an example of our uncritical acceptance of prodigies because we tend to dwell on the 1 or 2 successes, while quickly forgetting the millions of average children who started early and did not rise above the norm. Based on solid scientific data, it's time to correct this error in our thinking so I encourage parents to enjoy the inherent beauty of 3-, 4-, and 5-year-old imperfections.

Is Earlier Really Better?

The child prodigies that are famous throughout history weren't great because they began at an early age. As we have discussed, starting early isn't what caused their greatness. Instead, we should focus on the late bloomers from throughout history, since there are far more of those: Copernicus, Rembrandt, Bach, Newton, Beethoven, Kant, and Da Vinci, just to name a few. We know so much about the human brain and human cognition, and all of our knowledge goes against this instinct that "earlier is better." Yet it is still something we often believe we should continue to strive for.

We, as a society, are so impressed when "little people" can do something that seems beyond their years. As parents, we also have moments of doubt when we ask ourselves if our child should be able to accomplish a task or if there might be something wrong with our child. The boundaries between normal development, giftedness, and developmental delays can sometimes blur under such emotional pressure. Again, our lack of knowledge about how the brain functions can lead to these erroneous judgments. If your 2 1/2-year-old, for example, can talk in full sentences, does that make her smart? Or if your 3-year-old can recite the alphabet, does that mean he'll be an early reader? What about the 11-month-old who can sing the "A-B-C" song or the 2-year-old who can read you a bedtime story—which ones are gifted?

The Cart before the Proverbial Horse

A friend came over to my house with her 4-year-old son for a play date. The little boy looked at my water cooler and told me he could read what it said. "H-O-T—hot" he sounded out with an air of confidence. I could see the pride written all over his mother's face. This was indeed an accomplishment at the age of 4. I noted with great sadness that my 4-year-old had shown no interest in letters and sounds.

I asked the little boy why it would say "H–O-T—hot" on the water cooler, and he looked at me blankly. On further prompting, he managed a shoulder shrug. Suddenly, my son piped up, unperturbed by his illiteracy, and told us all in no uncertain terms that the water was hot so if you touch it, you might burn your hand and that you should stay away from it, at which point he promptly removed the other child's hand from the dripping tap!

Both children had so much to offer—one read and the other comprehended. Together they made a perfect pair! Both skills have their place in learning and cognitive growth. Should we prize one over the other? Should we teach one before the other?

A Frame of Reference . . .

Children develop differently, at different rates, and yet we love when someone strings together a model of development so that we know when our children are either meeting or missing their developmental milestones. Perhaps it's our collective need to believe that our children are ahead of the curve, or approximating the curve, or perhaps it's just the sheer existence of a curve that reassures us. G. Stanley Hall first identified those all-important developmental norms back in the 19th century; perhaps he had the foresight to anticipate our current educational climate or perhaps a teacher's role hasn't changed that much in over 100 years.

For parents, the amount of time between birth and kindergarten can feel long (as we are living through it day by day, minute by minute). Given our myopic view of our child's development, there may be a tendency among some of us to cling to any shred of evidence that our child is developing normally. Without any evidence to the contrary, or anyone to compare it to, we can mistakenly interpret normal development as gifted behavior. It is an understandable error since it is somewhat miraculous that our tykes virtually teach themselves to walk and talk!

It doesn't help that we are a nation obsessed with test scores and labels. By the end of those 60 long months, many parents are twitching in eager anticipation of those kindergarten test scores to validate their beliefs in their child's abilities, greatness, or normalcy. I remember my own doubts and fears about the kindergarten screening at our local school:

Kindergarten Didn't Go as Planned

Joshua, my pride and joy, was approaching the ripe old age of 5! It was almost kindergarten time. Both he and I were excited about the prospect of this new, previously uncharted territory. Joshua stared up at me, wide-eyed and innocent about this new adventure. I, too, was excited about the idea of my boy reaching this major milestone. I was also eager to learn more about American schools; after all, as a foreigner, I'd only seen them in the movies for 20+ years, and was now going to experience a real one.

Since he was 2, Joshua had been enrolled in a wonderful preschool program; you know the type: no sugar, no hitting, etc. Our philosophy at home matched the philosophy at preschool: use your words, play fair, and share. And, of course, we dispensed pearls of wisdom, such as "don't talk to strangers," "don't go out of the house by yourself," and "don't ever, ever eat anything that a stranger gives you," oh and "never, ever go with a stranger for any reason even if he says he's lost his doggie" (we all saw the *Oprah* special).

I'm still not sure whether it was because I was a foreigner, or a first-time mum, or a working mum (of course, it's possible it was because I was foreign and a first-timer and a working mum!); whatever the reason, kindergarten didn't go as planned. Though, I hasten to add, there was never a plan to begin with.

It all started with the "pre-kindergarten screening." Joshua was 4 years old at the time. Now, as you know, I am a developmental psychologist and, therefore, am not unfamiliar with the requirements for kindergarten or the screening process involved. This, as it turned out, was of no help whatsoever. We put on our cleanest clothes and, one morning in May, wandered up to our local school for this "pre-kindergarten screening," blissfully ignorant of what lay in store.

We registered at the desk then sat in the waiting area awaiting our turn. A woman a little older than myself came over to Joshua and asked him to follow her. She offered him her hand. Well, by this point, Joshua had memorized the rules: no hitting, no fighting (so far so good), and don't go with strangers. Joshua looked up at this woman as if she were half mad and told her in no uncertain terms that he was 4 years old and that she was a stranger and that he didn't go anywhere with strangers, ever! Good point, son.

We all agreed that it would be okay for Joshua to go with this "friend of Mum's" and that Mum would walk into the testing hall behind Joshua. So in we went, my rule-bound son, the stranger, and myself. I waited unobtrusively by the door as Joshua sat down at the testing table. I was, I must admit, just a little bit proud of my son for following his rules and questioning a stranger and somewhere, under all of the accompanying embarrassment, I felt like I had parented well those first 4 years.

Meanwhile, another storm was brewing. As I turned to leave the testing area, something caught my eye—in the center of the testing table was a bowl of candy, a large, round bowl overflowing with M&M's. I see, as only a mother can, the pained look on my son's face. It was certainly not test anxiety but rather the determination of a highly conscientious 4-year-old trying to resist this chocolate temptation. Joshua knew the rules, and this was most undoubtedly candy and these were, without a doubt, still strangers. I watched in quiet desperation as my son failed to answer question after question. Now we hadn't "studied" for the test, but I was reasonably confident that, even at the age of 4, he knew his name and could count to 10. I stood frozen at the door, watching his index and middle fingers twitch toward the bowl. I think I saw beads of sweat forming on his tiny brow.

I couldn't watch. I pried myself away from the testing area and returned to the waiting room. What kind of parent was I? What had I done to my son? If he had just eaten the candy and bounced off the walls like a normal child, all would've been fine. My mind was racing— would he begin his public school career in remediation? If he had just eaten the candy, then he would have heard the questions that were being asked. At least then I would be sure that he failed because he didn't know the answers instead of being preoccupied. Should I have prepared him better for the test? As I sat in that lonely waiting room, I realized that he didn't even know his own phone number. He'd never really needed to because it had never come up. He was 4 years old—he'd never had to call home from the mall or from a friend's house. He couldn't read, either. I thought that was the purpose of kindergarten, to teach them to read. Had I parented all wrong? I made up my mind that the second we left the testing center, I'd go home and teach him to read and count. Maybe the M&Ms hadn't mattered so much because how many questions could he have answered correctly anyway?

When he finally came out of the testing center, I was a mess. In the car, I "squeezed" him for information. Who's kidding who, on the walk to the car I began the inquisition. He couldn't write his name . . . He couldn't spell "cat" . . . He didn't know which number came after 10. He couldn't differentiate between the letters "P" and "F" . . . perhaps he belonged in remediation. Then again, what, realistically, should a 4-year-old be able to do? What should I have taught him to do? Tears were streaming down my face. I didn't need an exceptional child; I just wanted a normal child. I was wracked with guilt. What had I done, or not done, for my son?

* * *

Addendum to the cart and the proverbial horse:

"Little Joshua" is now the ripe old age of 26! I'm sure you'll be relieved to know that he did just fine at that kindergarten screening! He has now graduated, not only from kindergarten, but also from high school, university, and graduate school. Nonetheless, if you had shared those well-worn platitudes about "he'll be fine" or "you've raised him well" back on that fateful day, they would not have consoled me. Maternal love and parental determination are not governed by logic. This screening, as with so many other parenting moments, was fueled by raw emotion, and emotions, as we know, don't listen to reason.

Given that social comparison seems to be our frame of cognitive reference, it is easy to see why so many unsuspecting parents think early reading is the norm nowadays. Look at the stores, they are chock full of early literacy games and programs:

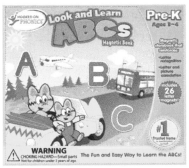

17 18

Some merchandise is cleverly labeled as an early lead, or a "jump start," on learning:

19

If you listen to the toys, they are promoting reading before our tots are even out of diapers. One program that was recently advertised on television claims that "your baby can read." It shows infants reading and responding to flash cards. It touts recent advances in our understanding of the human brain as one of the main reasons for the success of their program. Is it really possible that infants or toddlers can read? More importantly, if parents buy these products, will their infant or toddler become a reader? Perhaps our parents are motivated by fear: if every other infant is using this program, will their child be left behind?

20

21

You know that your baby can't read, that it is not developmentally appropriate to teach your baby to read, and, more importantly, that there is no good reason why a 6-, 8-, or 12-month-old infant would need to read. It did, however, take until July 2012 for the company to file for bankruptcy and until August 2012 for the litany of lawsuits to be settled.[22] "Your Baby Can Read" had to repay $185 million—their gross sales since 2008. While it is wonderful that justice was finally served, it is also alarming, from an educational perspective, that so many parents bought into this developmentally inappropriate notion. As "readiculous" as it sounds, we need to remind parents that their baby can't read and that this is not an educational goal we should strive for. We need to remind ourselves of the inherent beauty of a 1-year-old and the uniqueness of each age and stage of development.

As you well know, it's not just books and games that make these promises; there has been a proliferation of software and websites that has bombarded us lately as well.

23 24

It is easy to feel pressured by this commercialization of our deepest desire to give our children the best possible start in life. We do have this compunction to get a "jump start," if you will, on our children's learning. While there is certainly no harm in that, we need to get it right. Let's focus on the age-appropriate skills that we can nurture successfully.

MYTH:
"Your baby can read"
or "Earlier is better"

MYTH BUSTED:
Your baby can't and shouldn't read . . .

Your baby certainly cannot read. Just like a dog can lift his paw, your baby can learn a few rote responses, but your baby deserves better. Learning takes time. There are no educational shortcuts. There are no tricks—only refunds. The refund is for the money that you spent, but there is no refund for the precious time that you lost with your baby.

CHAPTER 4

MOZART, EINSTEIN, AND SHAKESPEARE IN THE BASSINET

MYTH:
"Listening to classical music (especially
Mozart) will make your child smarter . . ."

When well-intentioned parents start pushing their children from too young an age and begin formal instruction too soon, what exactly are they accomplishing from a cognitive perspective and how does it affect their child within the classroom?

Remembering Mozart and His Effect

Remember the "Mozart Effect"—listen to classical music and your child will be smarter? Wouldn't it be great if we could get smarter just by listening to music? Wouldn't it be even more fantastic if we could help our children become smarter just by playing music to them as they lie in their cribs? It's such a compelling story. We want to believe it and think of the corollary; no harm is done if it doesn't work! After all, no child was ever hurt by a little bit of Mozart, Beethoven, or Bach! We know that music is soothing and has plenty of emotional benefits, so why not embrace the notion that it makes us smarter? Let's face it, women have been singing to their babies since time began, so why not reap the cognitive benefits? But what exactly is this "Mozart Effect," and how did all the hype begin?

Watching the Mozart Effect? [25]

In 1993, a researcher by the name of Rauscher claimed that listening to classical music for brief periods could enhance your long-term and short-term spatial reasoning abilities. She completed the original study with her colleagues Shaw and Ky. The study, which appeared in the journal *Nature*, was called "Music and Spatial Task Performance." 448 college students participated in this study. After listening to 10 minutes of Mozart's Piano Sonata K, they were purported to have scored 8–10 IQ points higher on a spatial abilities test. They were 8–10 points better at mentally folding and cutting a snowflake in their heads! To add to the triviality of this finding, it wasn't

even a permanent improvement; it only lasted 10–15 minutes. So, folks, just think, if you want to improve your infant's mental snowflake-cutting skills for a quarter of an hour, then you have the perfect recipe! Oh, wait, you noticed I mentioned that Rauscher didn't test infants, right? She tested college students; well, maybe when your prodigy grows up you can hone those snowflake-cutting skills.

Rauscher's work did spur a slew of research and a great flurry of media activity. No one, not even Rauscher, however has been able to replicate her findings.[26] Rauscher claimed that these other studies were methodologically flawed, so some researchers even sought out Rauscher and Shaw,[27] who gave them detailed advice on how to design and execute their study to mirror the original findings, but to no avail.[28]

29

Why then are we discussing it at all? Because the Mozart Effect meets a functional need within our society. We want smarter children. We want quick and effortless methods to achieve this goal; hence a scientific legend was born and was quickly fueled by intense media hype.[30] Look no further than the parenting catalogs that arrive in your mailbox to confirm this belief. The Mozart Effect, which was hypothesized to be an auditory effect, is now available as a video or DVD for your neonate, infant, or toddler to enjoy. Look closely, maybe there is also a Shakespeare Effect and an Einstein Effect that has eluded researchers all this time.

31

Although there is no actual validity to The Mozart Effect, it hasn't stopped people from believing in it! In 1999, the governor of Georgia, Zell Miller, actually proposed spending $105,000 so that every newborn in his state could leave the hospital with a disc of classical music. From an emotional perspective, it certainly is a soothing idea, but Governor Miller, I'd hold off on adding more seats in those gifted classrooms . . .

32

The point to remember here is that there are no shortcuts and that growth and development take time. It is the quality interactions that you engage in with your child that often lead to the most successful outcomes.

The Mozart Effect is just one example of brain research that has been conducted over the past few years. Our understanding of the human brain has certainly advanced, but many of those advancements, as they relate to infants, toddlers, and preschoolers, only serve to reinforce our earlier theories and beliefs, not refute them.

The brain is a very complex organ and, although there is a great deal that we do not yet know about it, we know enough to separate fact from myth. For example, these facts are irrefutable:

- At birth, the human brain weighs a paltry 3 pounds.

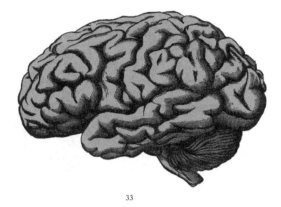

33

- At birth, the brain only weighs 25% of an adult's brain, but by the age of 2, the brain's weight has tripled to 75% of the weight of an adult's brain.

- A great deal of activity occurs in the brain during those first 2 years of life, making it seem like an ideal time to focus on learning. While this may be true, developmentally appropriate learning is key.

- The mechanism that contributes to cognitive growth, the neuron, is present from birth. We are born with at least 100 billion neurons in our brain.

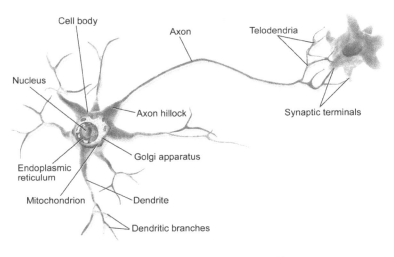

A Neuron in the Human Brain [34]

- In early infancy and toddlerhood, the human brain utilizes these 100 billion neurons by building connections that link information within the brain.

- These synaptic connections form "neural pathways" and are involved with organization and retrieval of information within the brain. This is where learning develops.

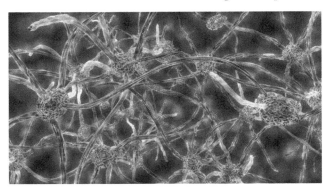

Neurons Connect to Each Other by Forming Synaptic Connections [35]

- The density of these neural connections intensifies within the first 2 years of life and is believed to be responsible for the change in brain mass. These synaptic connections form neural pathways that become an integral part of our thought processes or cognitions. Below is a scan of the density of these synaptic connections at birth, at 6 months of age, and at 2 years old.

- These neural pathways develop a "myelin sheath." This myelin sheath allows neural messages to be sent faster and with less interruption.

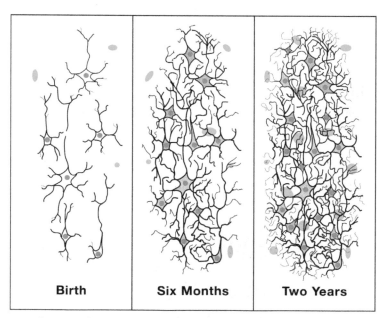

Birth   **Six Months**   **Two Years**

Synaptic Connections at Birth, 6 Months and 2 Years of Age

This rapid brain growth highlights the importance of early childhood education and the need for developmentally appropriate learning. We do, however, need to qualify what we mean by the connection between brain growth and "learning" and dispel some popular myths:

Usually when we think of growing, we think of increasing some component, but the brain actually undergoes a different type of growth. Between infancy and adulthood, we significantly reduce the number of synapses and neurons in our brain.[36] We call this process pruning. Pruning is like "downsizing." Unnecessary cells are weeded out or eliminated.[37] This is where experience plays a key role because the cells that survive this pruning process have been reinforced by experience. That experience includes hearing foreign languages or physically engaging with one's environment. The pruning process creates a more efficient system for transmitting the remaining impulses. Pruning begins shortly after birth and continues all the way through adolescence.[38]

The publicizing of this research on the pruning process has launched some parents into a frenzy of early childhood activities designed with the futile goal of attempting to prevent the brain from pruning. "Mommy and Me"–style classes have popped up all over the place, along with a craze to formally instruct children at a younger and younger age. Pruning is inevitable and can't be averted by an isolated 6-week Italian class for your 1-year-old or by a session of golf lessons for your 13-month-old! Perhaps fear of synaptic pruning is the motivating factor for some of these educational pursuits. Some parents mistakenly believe that their child will never be able to speak foreign languages, play a musical instrument, or learn to swim if these skills are not introduced before pruning sets in. Rest assured—formal instruction is not an essential component of brain development in the formative years. Learning occurs differently for all children.

How do we know when they are thinking, learning, myelinating or forming neural pathways?

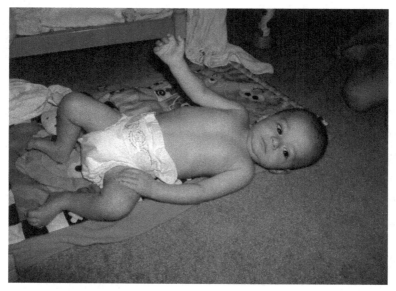

How do we know when they are thinking, learning, myelinating, or forming neural pathways?

Developmental psychologist Jean Piaget[39] wrote the most comprehensive theory of child development that we know of to date, despite never having access to these key neurological insights about the brain. He formed his theory of cognitive development based on what he saw, primarily by watching his own 3 children. His milestones map amazingly well to the scientific evidence that we now have of the developing brain. Based on this neurological and cognitive research, we can hypothesize about the best types of learning during early childhood:

We know that infants and toddlers are not little, slow adults. We cannot characterize their thinking as a slower version of adult thought. Young children think qualitatively different from adults. For example, ask a 2, 7, and 12-year-old the answer to the following question:

"What does 8+5 equal?"

It's not that the 12-year-old will think faster than the 2-year-old, rather that all 3 children will process the information differently.

- The 2-year-old will focus on numbers and probably repeat any number back to you (including pronouncing the numbers 80-20-1100 as one whole number "eightytwentyeleventy").

- The 7-year-old may rely on fingers to solve this math problem and offer 12, 13, or 14 as viable solutions, aware that a wrong answer may lead to embarrassment. 3 responses are an attempt to "hedge" or cover up this uncertainty and will often precede a distracting comment, such as, "Mum, did you get your hair cut today? It looks amazing."

- Meanwhile, the 12-year-old will probably look at you as if you're crazy and clearly insulting her intelligence since all 12-year-olds know that, and oh, so much more.

The point here is that thinking doesn't just get "faster" as we get older; it changes completely. Therefore, it isn't appropriate to ask a young child to think as we adults think.

In the first 2 years of life, according to Piaget, the brain learns through our senses and through exploration with the environment. This is not, then, the ideal time for formal instruction. It is a time to create an enriched setting for infants, toddlers, or preschoolers to interact with their environment through "hands on" manipulation.

What, then, are these children learning if they are engaging in formal instruction at such a young age? Even very young children can be taught to recite information, but there is a clear difference between the rote repetition of facts and the deeper understanding of information that leads to lifelong learning. We need to build solid educational foundations in early childhood so that they can sustain a child through kindergarten, elementary school, high school, college, and life.

MYTH:
"Listening to classical music (especially Mozart) will make your child smarter . . ."

MYTH BUSTED:
Listening to classical music won't make your child smarter, but it certainly is nice!

Although we want it to be true, the only scientific evidence that we have to date is that one group of college students were better able to mentally fold and cut a snowflake after they listened to classical music, but they were only better at this skill for 15 minutes.

It is interesting to note that the neural pathways that are involved in listening to classical music are the same neural pathways that we use for mathematical computation and higher-order thinking. It is not surprising, therefore, that people who are good at math enjoy classical music. However, listening to classical music has not been proven to have any causal effect on math skills to date.

Music is enjoyable to listen to; it can be relaxing and probably has many social and emotional benefits, so don't stop playing music, but unless you are looking to improve your snowflake-cutting skills, I doubt you'll see any cognitive benefits.

CHAPTER 5

WHY IS READING
SO DIFFICULT?

MYTH:
"Smaller words are easier to read"

In an effort to understand the complexities of the reading process, we need to take ourselves back to a time when reading posed a challenge to us. The exercises below are designed to help you see reading from a child's perspective. Let's look at reading through the eyes of a child.

Idiot Words

Try to read the words in Box 1 on the next page:

Read the words below:

DOG

PEN

RUN

YACHT

PHILISTINE

PTERODACTYL

Box 1

Are all of these words equally as easy to read? Obviously, if you are a novice reader, the longer words in Box 1 are harder to read than the shorter words. Now look at the words in Box 2 below. Are they easy to read?

Read the words below:

SON

THE

MY

ONE

EYE

LIGHT

Box 2

If you are 5 years old, what makes the words in Box 2 hard to read even though they are short words? For our novice reader, these words are so difficult to read because they violate basic decoding rules. If you try to "sound them out," they simply don't make sense. Phonetically, they are "unfriendly." We used to call them "idiot words" because they were idiotic! They just don't make sense according to the rules of phonics. So obviously word length alone cannot account for word difficulty.

The 5:18 Disconnect

Let's look more closely at our decoding expectations from a linguistic perspective. There are, as you know, 26 letters in the English language, but how many sounds (or phonemes) are there? You've probably figured out by now that there are obviously more than 26 sounds.

Actually, there are 45 sounds, or phonemes, in the English language! Let's break them down into vowels and consonants. We know that there are 5 vowels and 21 consonants, so how do we produce 45 sounds from 26 letters? The majority of this variety comes from our vowels. 5 little letters actually produce 18 different vowel sounds (count them in Box 3 if you want to double check my math!).

Since we've made the distinction between vowels and consonants, what actually is the difference? It's funny that we learn that there are 5 vowels (and can all name the letters) but can we easily articulate what a vowel actually is and what differentiates it from a consonant?

This might help:

The vowel sounds are the ones you can make while you brush your teeth because they are made by shaping an open mouth. Consonant sounds require the use of your speech organs (tongue, teeth, lips, hard palate, soft palate, etc.) so, for obvious reasons, you can't make consonant sounds while you brush your teeth! Try it!

---

45 phonemes or sounds = 18 vowel sounds + 27 consonant sounds

Vowel sounds as heard in:

TALL, PALMS, CURL, COOL, LEAVES, COULD, NOT, A, JUST, MAN, GET, IN, FIVE, HOUSES, JOIN, NEW, ROAD, WAY

Long monothongs: TALL, PALMS, CURL, COOL, LEAVES

Short monothongs: COULD, NOT, A, JUST, MAN, GET, IN

Dipthongs: FIVE, HOUSES, JOIN, NEW, ROAD, WAY

(Luck, 1975)

Box 3: The 5:18 Disconnect—5 Vowels and 18 Different Vowel Sounds

Now imagine you are 5 and just learning to read. You see an F (for fish), and every time you see an "F" it makes the same "f" sound. So far, so good? Consonants generally say their own name. They tend to be consistent, reliable staples in reading. Sometimes when you see a vowel, it also sounds like it should when it's sounded out—"a" as in "b-a-d," "e" as in "n-e-t," "i" as in "s-i-t," "o" as in "h-o-t," and "u" as in "s-u-n." But vowels are temperamental, they lack consistency, and they don't always sound the same each time that you meet them.

For example, sometimes you see an "a," and it could be an "a" as in "apple," or an "a" as in "harm," but sometimes it could also be an "a" as in "pay." How do you know which one to use? You, as an adult, just know from experience, but what does the average 5-year-old do? Phonics presents a long, hard road to decoding competence that is littered with nonsensical rules and frustrating exceptions. Yet this is how we choose to focus our children's activities during their formative years. This is what we narrowly define as reading.

This, however, is not new information. In 1965, the following poem appeared in the *New York Times*, and it makes the point far more eloquently than I can:

Hints on Pronunciation for Foreigners

I take it you already know
Of tough and bough and cough and dough?
Others may stumble but not you,
On hiccough, thorough, laugh and through.
Well done! And now you wish, perhaps,
To learn of less familiar traps?
Beware of heard, a dreadful word
That looks like beard and sounds like bird
And dead: It's said like bed, not bead
—For goodness' sake don't call it "deed"!
Watch out for meat and great and threat
(they rhyme with suite and straight and debt)
A moth is not a moth in mother
Nor both in bother, broth in brother
And here is not a match for there

Nor dear and fear for bear and pear.
And then there's does and rose and lose –
Just look them up—and goose and choose
And cork and work and card and ward
And font and front and word and sword
And do and go and thwart and cart
Come, come, I've hardly made a start!
A dreadful language? Man alive.
I'd mastered it when I was five!

(*Sunday New York Times*, January 1965)

Clearly there is more to reading than sounding out words—large or small. Given the 5:18 disconnect, words may be difficult to read!

MYTH:
"Smaller words are easier to read"

MYTH BUSTED:
Small words can be just as tricky
to read as longer words . . .

Dog and cat are small words with only 3 letters each. They are relatively easy to read. This does not, however, mean that all short words, are easy to read. Words such as "eye," "one," and "the" are all short words but they are not spelled the way they sound. They are not phonetically friendly words. This makes them extremely tricky words for a novice reader.

It is not the size of the word that determines its level of difficulty, per se, rather its phonetic friendliness and frequency of use that determines the "ease" with which it's read.

CHAPTER 6

THE FUNDAMENTAL FLAW

MYTH:
"You are cheating if you tell your children
words that they get 'stuck on,' and it
won't help them learn to read"

The Great Debate

The way that we teach reading is fundamentally flawed, but we've known that since at least the 1960s. Over the years, the massive failure rates in our classrooms have generated frequent debates about how reading should be taught. In the 70's, educators began what became known as "The Great Debate." This was a discussion about how to teach children to read. Phonics (saying the letters out loud), or decoding, was not working. Educators thought of a new strategy. They looked at how adults read and they tried to encourage children to simulate that process. It was called the "whole word approach." The whole word approach was based on the notion that when adults see a word, they say a word. Now go back to the previous chapter and ask yourself how you knew the words in Box 1. Did you "sound them out" or did you "see the word—say the word"? You saw the word and said it, right?

Lip Service

This sounded great! If adults did it, then children could be taught to do it too, right? Wrong! This backward thinking paid lip service to the years of effort that went into the automaticity of the reading process. Automaticity is the process by which we become so well practiced at a task that it requires less and less cognitive attention. Consider driving a car; the first time that you tried to drive, how much attentional energy did you put into pressing the accelerator and steering the wheel? How much did you focus on the cars that were behind, in front, and beside you? Could you simultaneously have turned on the radio, adjusted the air conditioning, and checked your GPS for directions? How about today when you drive a car? How many things do you do while driving? That is automaticity! When you automate the lower-level functions, you free up more cognitive capacity to focus on other areas.

Reading in a Flash

The same is true for reading. Once you have figured out the names of the letters and become familiar with basic sounds, letter combinations, and, of course, the ever-present exceptions, then you can dedicate more of your attention to other matters. The point here is that automaticity takes time.

This brings us back to our "great debate," where well-intentioned educators began teaching children to "recognize words" in order to encourage automaticity. And, thus, the flash card era began! This was the birth of the "whole word" approach to reading: see a word—say a word.

Think about it—how could a child who has no clues to work with recognize a word on a flash card that he or she has never seen before? Even if, through rote memorization, you learn several words on several flash cards, what do you do when you see a new word that you're unfamiliar with? Herein lies the problem with the whole word approach: it doesn't provide a strategy for children to read novel words; it only allows them to identify familiar words. Obviously, some words are "sight words" for children. It would be difficult to find an average 4-year-old child who doesn't recognize a "McDonald's" sign or a "STOP" sign here in America.

The Debate Rages On

So the Great Debate rages on . . . or does it? How is reading taught today? Choosing which strategy to teach children to read has become "the most politicized topic in the field of education."

Small Words, Big Print, Easy Read, Right?

Given the complexity of the English language and the cognitive capacity of the average 3- to 5-year-old, we should use books that contain "phonetically fair" words, i.e. words that spell the way they sound. This would allow our inexperienced readers to be more successful at this aspect of reading comprehension. Decoding seems to be such a vital part of learning to read, although it is certainly not the whole story.

Seek out books that have words that are phonetically fair! Use this rule as your first gauge to determine if a book is suitable for a novice reader. It doesn't matter if the words are small or the print is big; it matters if your child can successfully decode what is printed. I love Dr. Seuss and his cats in hats, etc. If you can't find enough books, then make your own: "Sam Can!" and "Matt Sat!" to name but a few! Phonetically fair words are just easier for novice readers to master.

There seems to be this mistaken belief that telling your child words that he or she may be struggling with is somehow tantamount to cheating. This is stuff and nonsense. Helping your children master "phonetically unfriendly words" will help them conquer the reading process.

Telling your child the correct pronunciation of a word is an ideal reading strategy. This takes some of the frustration out of reading aloud, and it makes reading a more pleasurable experience for both you and your child. Words that aren't phonetically fair or don't spell the way that they sound are too difficult for a novice reader. These words can't be decoded and are unintelligible to novice readers, so although it may feel like it, it's not really cheating! In the long run, it is far better to create a love for reading than to turn it into a chore that children dread.

MYTH:
"You are cheating if you tell your children
words that they get 'stuck on,' and it
won't help them learn to read"

MYTH BUSTED:
Tell your children the "difficult words" and
put some fun back into reading together . . .

So . . . Is that it?

So, is that it? Use phonics, whole word, or some personalized combination, tell your child the words he or she doesn't know, and then bingo, your child is a reader? What does it mean to be a "reader"? Is it knowing your ABCs? Is it being able to say the words out loud or decoding them? Or is it more than that?

CHAPTER 7

BUT WAIT ... THERE'S MORE

MYTH:
"If children can repeat it out loud,
then they understand it"

W e've known for years that there's more to the story than decoding. Yet many of us spend our children's precious preschool years, if not the first 5 years of our children's lives, fixated on this concept. As a first step to decoding, we focus on teaching our children the names of the letters; we have songs about them, preschools devoted to them, and television shows spouting them. Ironically, however, according to the research, teaching children the names of letters does not give them any appreciable advantage when they finally crack that code and learn to read.[40] So why is it that we are still so narrowly focused on knowing the names of the letters and teaching our tots to decode?

Sometimes we mistakenly believe that decoding is the only, the first, or the most important aspect of reading, but as the following chapters will explain, that is far from true. This is the fundamental flaw in teaching reading to children.

Igneous Fusion

We have been making mistakes in our educational practices for many years. William James,[41] considered to be the founding father of education, wrote about one of our earlier mistakes in knowledge and learning:

He went to visit a colleague who happened to be a teacher. He sat in on this colleague's class. The teacher seemed delighted with his students, who all raised their hands to answer a seemingly well-rehearsed question that was being asked in the classroom. The teacher asked the students:

"In what condition is the interior of the globe?"

Each student that was called on to answer gave a well-recited response:

"The condition of the interior of the globe is igneous fusion."

All the students appeared to have learned to recite a standard answer. On the surface, it appeared that all the students knew the answers. William James asked if he could address the students. His friend was delighted. Instead of the standard questions that the teacher had posed, James asked the students:

"Suppose you should dig a hole in the ground, hundreds of feet deep, how should you find it at the bottom, warmer or colder than on top?"

None of the students could answer his question. The teacher intervened on behalf of the students. He explained to James that he was not wording the question correctly. The teacher then again asked the students, "In what condition is the interior of the globe?" All the students' hands shot up in the air . . .

James used this example to illustrate the difference between reciting information and true knowledge or understanding.

Clearly, if the students had understood the term "igneous fusion" in relation to the core of the earth and temperature, then they would have known whether it was hot or cold down there regardless of the wording of the question!

William James (1842–1910)[42]

William James maintained that this classic mistake in education needed to be addressed. He believed that he had learned more from the conversations around his dinner table than from any teacher or course that he had taken. He was referring to the risk-free, non-judgmental environment involving the frank exchange of ideas with his family versus the standardized and clinical setting of formal education where much of the learning is rote memorization and there is little room for debate, creativity, and true understanding.

MYTH:
"If children can repeat it out loud,
then they understand it"

MYTH BUSTED:
If children can repeat it out loud, they
don't necessarily understand it

Just because children can say the words out loud, it doesn't mean that they understand what they are saying.

There is a key difference between the "rote repetition of facts" and the deeper underlying understanding of concepts. True learning involves more than just repetition.

CHAPTER 8

SETTING THEM UP TO FAIL

EMPHASIZING THE MYTH:
"If your child can say the words out
loud, then your child can read"

The premise that decoding should be the key emphasis for early reading is fundamentally flawed. It is based on the assertion that reading has a predetermined sequence. It presupposes that we identify the words associated with the letters on the page and, when this becomes fluent, we focus on the development of comprehension skills so that we can actually understand what we are reading.[43] While this seems to be a standard model for reading,[44] it suggests a sequential pattern to the reading process that is counterintuitive. It implies that we learn to decode words or say the words out loud, and then (and only then) do we add meaning to those words through comprehension.

Grim Determination

Yet this is how we teach reading in many of our preschools, kindergartens, child care centers, and homes. In our grim determination to teach our children to read, we focus very narrowly on the letters and sounds. Understanding, or comprehension, takes a back seat as we teach the names of the letters in an environment that is often devoid of meaning. This may not be the best approach. It appears to sell our children short and is setting them up to fail. It can lead to the misguided belief that once they have read the words out loud, then their job is done.

Pay Attention!

We have now isolated our first problem: It seems that our children are not paying enough attention to the material that they are reading. But this is not new information; we have known this since the 1970s. According to the research, between 50–95% of third- and sixth-grade children failed to notice when blatant errors were included in stories.[45] One such story described how dark it was at the bottom of the ocean because there was absolutely no light, yet fish down there only ate red food! Children failed to notice this massive inconsistency in the story—that fish couldn't see the color of their food in the pitch dark. You can read the fish story for yourself in Box 4.[46]

> Many different kinds of fish live in the ocean. Some fish have heads that make them look like alligators and some have heads that make them look like cats. Fish live in different parts of the ocean. Some fish live near the surface of the water, but some fish live way down at the bottom of the ocean. There is absolutely no light at the bottom of the ocean. Some fish that live at the bottom of the ocean know their food by its color. They will only eat red fungus.
>
> (Markman, 1979)

Circumventing Grice

Now, before you go explaining away these reading problems as ambiguous information or plausible if the food had a smell or was fluorescent, or there was only red food in the area to begin with, let me assure you that any child who came up with even a semi-plausible explanation was scored as correct in this study. The 50–95% failure rate referred to children who, when asked to verify that the story made sense, failed to notice any problem at all. If you're thinking to yourself, "I bet that Grice's Cooperative Principle is at play here," you might be right. This principle suggests that children ostensibly believe that the information that they are presented with will always be true and accurate. This would cause children to try to make sense of the inconsistent information even if they didn't verbalize their attempts. To circumvent this problem, or principle, children were warned that there was a problem with the stories.[47] An example of such instructions read something like this:

"Some of the essays have problems with them. A problem is something that might confuse people or something that people might have trouble understanding."[48]

Since the questions that the children were asked were so important in ascertaining whether or not they noticed the inconsistent information, I have detailed the entire set of questions that were used in the fish story. These questions are called "probe questions." Box 5 contains these probe questions.

Probe Questions to Determine If Children Noticed Inconsistencies

- What do you think?
- Do you have any questions?
- Did I forget to tell you anything?
- Did everything make sense?
- Can you tell me everything you learned about fish?
- Did everything make sense?
- Is there any light at the bottom of the ocean?
- Can fish see without light?

(Markman & Gorin, 1981)

Box 5 Probe Questions to Determine Comprehension

Doubting Thomases

For the "Doubting Thomases" among you, and I know you are out there, try reading the story in Box 6 called "A Snowy Day." Read it, and then we'll discuss it.

It had been snowing all afternoon, but it was not yet cold enough for the pond at the bottom of the yard to freeze over with ice. Tiddles the cat sat by the front door patiently waiting for someone to let her back into the warm house. She had been outside all afternoon watching the children, Tim and Lisa, playing in the snow. The children had wanted to skate on the fishpond, but since it was not cold enough for the pond to freeze, they had built a snowman instead. They were delighted with their snowman that now stood beside the old pine tree. Having finished their snowman, the children were now skating happily across the fishpond while the fish jumped in and out of the water. Tiddles looked at the fish and dreamed of dinner.

(Rubman & Waters, 2000)

Box 6—A Snowy Day

Skating on Thin Water

Now you tell me, how can children skate on a pond that isn't frozen? How can fish jump in and out of the water if the pond is frozen? So, we certainly have ourselves some inconsistencies

65

here![49] How did the children fare? How many of them spotted these blatant mistakes?

Third and sixth graders are usually tested in these types of studies, and this study was no exception. How many third-grade children do you think noticed that the children were skating while the fish were jumping? In this (and similar stories), around 30% of the third-grade children identified the inconsistency (in any way, shape, or form). Do you think that the sixth graders did any better? After all, they are older. Well, you would be right: 44% of sixth-grade students noticed the problem. A little reality check here—that means that more than half of the 11- and 12-year-old children who read a simple story couldn't detect a massive theoretical problem within that story.

Too Nitpicky?

This whole "inconsistency detection paradigm" may all seem a little nitpicky to you. After all, does it really matter if a child notices an obvious error in a story? Does that really mean that the child can't read? Well, that depends on how you define "reading." Research is littered with many different types of examples of comprehension failure. Entire story endings have been switched so that the character in the story that went to the dentist, for example, ended up with a haircut.[50] This should really confirm any remaining suspicions that our children have a reading problem.

Don't Look Back

Looking more closely at what children do when they read these types of stories, it appears that younger children don't "look back" or reread the text. This suggests, yet again, that they are not even processing a potential problem. We could try just telling them to look back, or reread. This type of advice is called "metacognitive" and, believe it or not, it actually works! Just telling children to pay attention and look back in the story really does improve their reading comprehension slightly.[51] Slightly, but not enough.

MYTH
"If your child can say the words out loud, then your child can read"

MYTH BUSTED AGAIN!
Don't assume that just because they can read it aloud that they are also comprehending what they are reading.

When so many of our students fail to notice blatant errors in stories such as fish seeing in the dark or children skating on water, we have to concede that there is a problem. Saying the words out loud does not guarantee comprehension competence. Without comprehension, our children are functionally illiterate, just like the 42 million adult Americans who cannot follow the directions on a can of soup. The "fish and skating" research was conducted in the 1970s. That was over 40 years ago. It's time to reinvent the reading process to ensure that all of our children can make their own soup someday.

CHAPTER 9

EARLIER JUST ISN'T BETTER

MYTH:
"Short sentences are easier to understand"

AND BONUS MYTH:
"Children learn better when they read
to you, not when you read to them"

When we teach young children to read, we run into an "availability" problem. The younger the child, the less "cognitive capacity" that child tends to have. While our capacity increases as we grow older, it is severely limited in early childhood. This is a serious deterrent in reading comprehension since true reading, reading for meaning, places a huge cognitive demand on the reader. Let's look more closely at the other requirements for successful reading comprehension.

A Reading Proposition

Decoding, in all its various forms, can be summarized as "Lexical Access." Lexical access is just one of several components in the reading comprehension process.[52] This process describes a combination of strategies that develop simultaneously. The other components include "proposition assembly" and "proposition integration."[53] Let's look at these in terms of children's literature.

Let's assume that, using whatever means possible, our children can now recite the words on a page. Whether the emphasis was on decoding, or the whole word approach, or a combination of the two, let's assume that our children can now verbalize the printed word. How do our children now make sense of that text? If we look more closely at the printed word, we can see that it is made up of a collection of propositions that are combined together to form meaning.

A proposition is an idea unit. "Proposition assembly" is the way these propositions, or idea units, are stacked in a story. Proposition integration is the combination of idea units within a phrase, sentence, or paragraph. Let's make up a story together.

There was a car (one proposition). It was old (proposition 2). It was red (proposition 3). It crawled (proposition 4). It went slowly (proposition 5). It went up the hill (proposition 6).

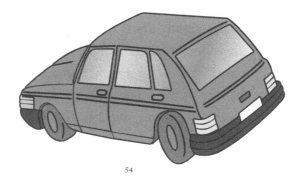

54

We can combine all 6 propositions into one sentence:
"The old, red car crawled slowly up the hill."

Or we can separate out the idea units to help a beginning reader learn how to integrate ideas:

There was a car. It was old. It was red. It went slowly. It crawled. It went up the hill.

Bear in mind as well that a great deal of a novice reader's attentional energy or cognitive capacity is being utilized in the decoding process, so we might want to simplify the number of propositions in a sentence. While the sample sentence "The old, red car crawled slowly up the hill" is actually quite short, it contains 6 idea units or propositions.

The point here is that, just as word length alone does not account for reading difficulty in the decoding process, sentence length alone does not account for comprehension difficulty. It is the number of propositions in a sentence that determine the complexity of comprehension.

Now take a fresh look at the books that you are reading with your children. Are the propositions simple and easy to assemble? Does the story build slowly to allow the child time to create a visual representation while simultaneously trying to decode the words to read aloud? It would be great if children's books were measured in their complexity by the number of integrated propositions in one sentence rather than the number of words or the size of the font! Take, for example, Dr. Seuss, one of my favorite children's authors. Look at the first few pages of *Green Eggs and Ham*.[55]

"I am Sam. Sam I am. I do not like that, Sam I am. Do you like green eggs and ham? I do not like them, Sam I am. I do not like green eggs and ham."

Dr. Seuss actually assembles and integrates nonsense propositions with you!

MYTH:
"Short sentences are easier to understand"

MYTH BUSTED:
Short sentences just aren't easier to understand!

It is not the length of the sentence, per se, that makes it simple or complex. It is the number of propositions within a sentence that determines the complexity.

"The little, red car crawled slowly up the steep hill" may be a short sentence, but because it contains 6 ideas or propositions, it is not so easy to understand. Rather than looking at sentence length, per se, we should focus on the number of propositions contained within each sentence.

Through the Eyes of a Child

To simulate the process by which children integrate, or fail to integrate, propositions, try the "lateral thinker" in Box 6.

A man was born before his father,
killed his mother and married his sister.
Yet he is considered normal by all who knew him.
How come?

(Sloane & Machale, 1997)

Box 6—A Lateral Thinker

Why was this puzzle so difficult to understand and solve? After all, each proposition within the puzzle made sense in isolation, e.g. "there was a man," "he was born," "he killed his mother," etc. It is only when you combine these propositions that they fail to make sense. To the best of my knowledge, normal men aren't born before their fathers, they don't kill their mothers, and they certainly don't marry their sisters! If this puzzle fails to make sense to you (as it should), then you are integrating your propositions. Now, I am not suggesting for one minute that we give young children strange puzzles to test their integration rates; rather that this is an example of how much work you put into the reading process in terms of proposition integration.

Choice A—3 One-Dollar Bills   *Choice B—1 Ten-Dollar Bill*

56

To explain this man, think of an infant born in front of his father in the delivery room, where his mother died in childbirth. This same man grew up to become a priest and performed the marriage ceremony whereby his sister married her husband. Now reread Box 6. Does the man seem more normal now?

Because you tried to integrate these propositions, the story failed to make sense to you. When children are confused by a story or it doesn't make sense to them, this is evidence that they are attempting to integrate propositions. This is confirmation that our children are actively engaging in the comprehension process and that they are beginning to extract meaning from print. This is wonderful! This is also an ideal time to focus on reading to your children. This will free up their cognitive capacity to focus on comprehension rather than "lexical access" or decoding.

BONUS MYTH:
"Children learn better when they read
to you, not when you read to them"

BONUS MYTH BUSTED:
You can free up some cognitive capacity
for a child if you decode for them.

Although it's important that children practice reading aloud, it is also important for them to practice integrating propositions so that they can make sense of the printed word. When you read to children, you allow them the luxury of focusing their attentional energy on the meaning of the story. This is an ideal time to work on comprehension skills. We should, therefore, read to our children on a regular basis to allow them the opportunity to build textual meaning through proposition integration.

CHAPTER 10
THINK AS A CHILD THINKS

MYTH:
"Telling children facts will make them smarter"

During the preschool years, our children have other cognitive issues that impede their comprehension skills. Children in the preschool years are in a stage of cognitive development termed "preoperational thought."[57] Children between 2 and 7 years are limited in their thinking. These preoperational children are "egocentric." This does not mean that they are selfish, rather that they don't have enough cognitive capacity to take on any perspective other than their own. This egocentricity is evident in many domains of a child's life. In speech, young children often appear to be talking *to* another child, but if you listen closely, they are actually talking *at* each other, holding 2 independent conversations that don't involve any interaction!

An Example of Egocentric Communication

Blankie

Jean Piaget, the father of developmental psychology, also described children's perspective-identifying as egocentric. He believed that young children lacked the capacity to take on another person's perspective because they were using all of their available resources to focus on their own perspective. This accounts for little Billy bringing you his blankie when he perceives that you are sad. When Billy is sad, he is comforted by his blankie so, similarly, if you are sad, Billy's blankie will comfort you!

Egocentric Perspective Taking
Billy's Blanket Will Comfort You as It Comforts Him[58]

Parental Temptation

There is always the parental temptation to tell children the correct answer or give them facts, instead of allowing them to discover them for themselves. This glosses over these cognitive limitations and appears to solve the problem. Everyday interactions with our children can reveal that these problems and limitations are definitely not solved:

When was the last time you gave a child money as a gift? Look at the Box below. Which do you think a child would prefer, Choice A or Choice B?

Choice A is a gift of 3 one-dollar bills, while choice B is 1 ten-dollar bill. Young children, as you know, prefer the 3 one-dollar bills. Somehow, in their preoperational minds, they think that 3 is more than the single ten-dollar bill. This makes sense to them because 3 is more than 1, regardless of what each of the 3 contain or how much value the 1 has!

This error occurs because preoperational thinking also falls prey to what Piaget called "centration." This is the idea that children center, or fixate, on one feature of a task and fail to consider other perceptual features. This causes the child to lack the ability to "conserve." This problem happens with solids, liquids, and matter. While, according to Piaget, this is an error that we outgrow, be honest with yourself—have you ever poured leftovers into a container only to discover that they don't all fit? Hard as you try, you can't seem to mash them in so that the lid can close! This is the same principle. It is called conservation of matter!

Fixing These Mistakes

Another mistake that some adults make is in our understanding of the root cause of these "errors" in thinking. Many well-intentioned adults try to talk their way through these errors in children's thinking. They try to explain to a child that although 3 looks like more than 1, $10 is actually more than $3. They even ask their child to repeat this out loud. This creates an "illusion of knowledge" whereby parents believe that telling a child the correct answer will also (somehow) give that child the deep, underlying understanding that should accompany it. Just saying that "Choice B" is better doesn't make it so in the mind of a 5-year-old. They can repeat your words aloud, they can even take the correct bill, but have you changed their thinking? This is why children need to interact with their environment to learn. They need the feedback. They need to discover for themselves. Telling is not the same as doing. Children will outgrow these conservational errors as they interact more with the environment and as they develop more cognitive capacity.[59]

Classic Mistakes

To demonstrate that children's thinking is not changed simply by telling them what to say, a study was designed to test this concept of conservation and verbal communication. You may be familiar with Piaget's famous water study[60] where he poured water from one tall, thin beaker into a short, wide container. Children who saw the water being poured claimed that the tall, thin beaker had more water since the water line was higher. It was obvious to any adult that it was the same amount of water in both beakers. Yet children in the preoperational stage were misled by the physical height of the water in the beakers. To them, taller is more, just like 3 is more than 1. Preoperational children repeatedly chose Beaker A as the correct response claiming that it had more water than Beaker B despite the fact that they watched the water being poured from one container to the other!

Piaget's Classic Conservation of Water Task
(It's not a cognitive problem, it's a linguistic issue.)

Is it possible that children understand these concepts, but they have a limited vocabulary so they can't verbalize their thoughts? One research team wanted to test whether children just lacked the verbalization skills or whether this was a cognitive miscommunication. They tried to train children in the language of conservation.

Using the same beaker example, they trained children to explain the answer with a response like, "There is the same amount of water in both beakers, you just poured it. Beaker A is tall and thin so it looks like it has more water than Beaker B, which is long and low." The children were then tested after being trained in their responses. The majority of children who were tested gave the correct verbal response: "There is the same amount of water in each beaker, you only poured the water; you didn't change the amount of water." This sounded like a success, but when children were asked to take the beaker with the most water, they consistently took Beaker A, the tall, thin beaker with the higher water level! Why did this happen? Because you can train a child to talk and to recite information, but that doesn't change their underlying cognitive processing.

This is what we need to focus on in education. It is time that we start to value the underlying thinking instead of just the verbalization. This study beautifully demonstrates that "saying it" is not the same as "believing it."

We Cannot Impose Knowledge on a Child

As adults, we do not make these errors. To allow children's thinking to mature, time and interaction with their environment will slowly change their thought processes. In the meantime, we should focus on more cognitively appropriate activities.

It is tempting to believe that telling our children information will make them smarter, but repeating someone else's verbalization only creates the "illusion of knowledge," whereas exploration and discovery create an underlying understanding. By constructing knowledge, children build a solid educational foundation that will sustain them throughout their academic travels and their lives.

Thinking Errors

What a state!

I was at a mother's playgroup many years ago with my now 23-year-old, then 3-year-old, son. At one particular meeting of this playgroup, one of the mothers mentioned out loud and with great pride, to no one in particular, that her son (also aged 3) could name all 50 states. I was impressed. The whole group seemed impressed. Then I began to think about it. Why would a 3-year-old child need to know all 50 states? I got lost in my own thoughts and began to wonder if he even knew what the abstract concept of a state was, and what a state would mean to a 3-year-old anyway? Having performed his party trick and recited all 50 states, I later asked this little 3-year-old what a state was. He gave me a look that somehow conveyed a mixture of confusion, innocence, and utter disregard, kicked me in the shin, and then promptly ran away!

Did he know what a state was? That wasn't the point; the point was, and continues to be, that at the young age of 3, states, especially all 50, don't matter in the life of a child the way they matter to an adult. This mother should indeed have been proud that her son could remember 50 of anything at such a young age, but from a cognitive perspective, focusing your attention on what matters most to a child will help them form deeper connections.

MYTH:
"Telling children facts will make them smarter"

MYTH BUSTED:
Telling children facts will not make them smarter
unless you address the deeper underlying meaning
in a developmentally appropriate context

Superficial and rote repetition sells our children short.

It is impressive when young children tell us something that we did not expect them to know. It is much less impressive when they don't actually know what they are saying. Superficial knowledge sells our children short. It is not a good use of their valuable time, and this information does not stand the test of time—it is a cheap party trick compared to the deeper underlying cognition that accompanies true understanding.

CHAPTER 11

PICTURE THIS!

MYTH:
"It is cheating to look at the pictures to
figure out what the words say or mean"

Sometimes we need a little extra help in our attempt to comprehend a text and integrate those propositions. Another useful strategy in proposition integration development is the use of pictures. Read the story in Box 7 below:

If the balloons popped, the sound would not be able to carry since everything would be too far away from the correct floor. A closed window would also prevent the sound from carrying since most buildings tend to be well insulated. Since the whole operation depends on a steady flow of electricity, a break in the middle of the wire would also cause problems. Of course the fellow could shout, but the human voice is not loud enough to carry that far. An additional problem is that a string could break on the instrument. Then there could be no accompaniment to the message. It is clear that the best situation would involve less distance. Then there would be fewer potential problems. With face to face contact, the least number of things could go wrong.

(Bransford & Johnson, 1972)

Box 7 The Importance of Pictures

Now rate the story that you just read in Box 7 for comprehensibility on a scale from 1–7, where 7 is highly comprehensible. Now try to retell the story in your mind. As a skilled reader, you probably tried to make sense of the story in Box 7, but I'm sure it was just a little frustrating. Also, as a skilled reader, you probably recalled some facts, but it probably

Bransford & Johnson, 1972

felt like there was something missing. How did you rate the story? When students were asked to rate the same story on the same scale, they rated it around 2.3 out of 7 possible points for comprehensibility.[61] Now look at the picture on the next page and reread the story in Box 7.

If the balloons popped, the sound would not be able to carry since everything would be too far away from the correct floor. A closed window would also prevent the sound from carrying since most buildings tend to be well insulated. Since the whole operation depends on a steady flow of electricity, a break in the middle of the wire would also cause problems. Of course the fellow could shout, but the human voice is not loud enough to carry that far. An additional problem is that a string could break on the instrument. Then there could be no accompaniment to the message. It is clear that the best situation would involve less distance. Then there would be fewer potential problems. With face to face contact, the least number of things could go wrong.

(Bransford & Johnson, 1972)

Box 7 The Importance of Pictures

Why is the story so much easier to comprehend and recall when the picture accompanies it? The picture helps you organize the individual propositions within the story and it allows you to integrate the idea units into a meaningful whole. Using the same 7-point scale, how would you rate the comprehensibility of the passage in conjunction with the picture? The average comprehension rate was 6.1 for students who read the story and saw the picture[62]—a far cry from the 2.3 for the pictureless story.

When students were shown the picture after they had read the story, it didn't seem to help their comprehension. It was only when the picture was shown in conjunction with the story that comprehension was enhanced. Think about this when evaluating children's storybooks. Is there an appropriate picture, and does it appear at the most opportune time as the text is being read?

What about the multitude of children's storybooks that have pictures but the picture does not really mirror the story? It may only contain aspects of the story, like some of the characters. Will that type of pictorial representation enhance comprehension?

When students were shown pictures that contained all the elements of the story, but the relationship among the objects was not clarified, comprehension did not improve.

The students who saw this type of picture that did not correspond to the text rated it as a 3.7/7 for comprehensibility (remember that the correct picture group scored an average of 6.1 and the no picture group scored an average of 2.3 on the 7-point comprehension scale).[63]

Partial context for balloon passage
Bransford & Johnson, 1972

It is not the picture itself that enhances the comprehension and recall of a story, but the organization of the related items in the picture. When students were asked to recall what they had read, the students who saw the contextually correct picture recalled an average of 8 ideas from the story; those who saw the objects in the partial context picture that did not match the text recalled an average of 4 ideas; and the students who heard the story without any pictorial representation recalled an average of 3.6 ideas from the story. In other words, the picture should be an exact depiction of the events in the story if it is to be used as an optimal comprehension tool.

Based on this research, there is a suggestion here that we should find storybooks for our novice readers that have pictures that relate to the actual content of the story and that portray the contextual relationships within the story rather than just the characters or setting. This would reinforce the interrelationship of the characters and objects in the story in pictorial form as the story is being read to our children or as they are trying to read for themselves. If you are in any doubt about the value of accurate pictures that describe the relationship among items, buy some IKEA furniture and try to assemble it yourself using only the wording on the instruction sheet!

Here are 3 "picture points" to check in your home: first, make sure that your books have pictures; second, make sure that the pictures match the action in the story; and finally, make sure that you don't slap your hand over that precious image.

MYTH:
"It is cheating to look at the pictures to figure out what the words say or mean"

MYTH BUSTED:
Looking at the pictures can help a child integrate propositions and extract meaning from a printed text.

Some parents mistakenly believe that allowing their child to look at the pictures is somehow cheating. It is not; so to all those teachers who put their hand across the picture to prevent their children from seeing the image—think again. This picture is a great example for your child. It shows your child what he or she should be picturing or mentally representing. It is an invaluable demonstration of the correct image for them to picture, assuming, of course, that the action in the picture matches the action in the story.

CHAPTER 12

INFER WHAT YOU WILL . . .

MYTH:
If children can "sound out" the words,
then children can "read"

Reading often involves extracting meaning that isn't explicitly printed on the page. This often involves the inference-making process. It is often more difficult for children to make inferences rather than to recall a story through rote memorization.[64] They really have to work hard to think about the information that they are given. Preschoolers were tested to examine how well they could make inferences about familiar stories. The children, aged 3 to 4 years old, were read a nursery rhyme. They were asked questions that tapped into their ability to recall the text and their ability to make inferences about the text. Recall questions allowed them to literally quote the nursery rhyme in their response, whereas inference-based questions required them to generate their own novel response. For example, in the rhyme "Little Miss Muffet," children are asked what frightened Miss Muffet away. To answer this question, children need only quote the rhyme "along came a spider . . . and frightened Miss Muffet away." Whereas the inference-based question—"what was Miss Muffet afraid of?"—requires the reader to rethink the story.

Little Miss Muffet

Little Miss Muffet sat on her tuffet
eating her curds and whey.
Along came a spider and sat down beside her
and frightened Miss Muffet away.

Recall vs. Inference Questions

Recall: What frightened Miss Muffet away?
Inference: What was Little Miss Muffet afraid of?

Sample Nursery Rhymes with Questions Based
on Rote Memorization or Inference

Children were much more successful at answering the rote recall question than the inference-based question.

To enhance inference-making skills, some of the children acted out the nursery rhymes. Acting out the rhymes significantly enhanced the likelihood that children would respond correctly to the inference-based question. It is possible that acting out the story reduced the cognitive auditory load and allowed children to focus more on the story content. Remember, these were pre-readers, so while no actual reading was involved for the children participating in this study, look at the cognitive gains from acting out the rhymes. Again, children need encouragement to actively engage in the comprehension process.

MYTH:
If children can "sound out" the words,
then children can "read"

MYTH BUSTED:
Decoding isn't reading—it's saying the words
out loud. Reading requires comprehension.

CHAPTER 13

WHEN REREADING DOESN'T HELP

MYTH:
"Academic programs that focus on learning the ABCs and reading short words are more valuable than programs that focus on play"

If we are to successfully combine meaning with early literacy, then we have our work cut out for us. There are 3 key components that the reader brings to a text. We are going to look at the role of background knowledge, schematic access, and the reader's perspective.

Keep It in the Background

Let's begin our discussion of background knowledge by reading the story in Box 8:

Jim went to the restaurant and asked to be seated in the gallery. He was told that there would be a half hour wait. Forty minutes later, the applause for his song indicated that he could proceed with the preparation.

Twenty guests had ordered his favorite, a cheese soufflé. Jim enjoyed the customers in the main dining room. After 2 hours, he ordered the house specialty—roast pheasant under glass. It was incredible to enjoy such exquisite cuisine and yet still have fifteen dollars. He would surely come back soon.

(Schank & Abelson, 1975)

Box 8—The Importance of Background Knowledge

The problems with this story go way beyond proposition integration! The story seems to violate just about every preexisting norm that you may have about restaurants and simply doesn't make sense!

Let's walk through the story together. "Jim went to the restaurant." So far so good, but why did he ask to be seated in a gallery? Restaurants don't have galleries. Oh! Maybe they meant "balcony"; we can overlook that. "He was told there would be a half hour wait"—been there! But here we run into some trouble: "Forty minutes later the applause for his song . . ." What song? He's in a restaurant, isn't he? "He could proceed with the preparations." What preparations? It's a restaurant, isn't it?

Herein lies the point of the story. Look how hard you are working! Look at what you are bringing from past experiences to the story. This is referred to as "background knowledge." It refers to all the additional information that you bring with you as you try to make sense of a text. It is what you see when you read "between the lines." This is your schematic knowledge.[65] Schematic knowledge is the foundation of our understanding. It helps us to clarify, organize, and interpret information.

When you read the name "Jim," you probably accessed all your knowledge of men, "Jims" in particular! Next you found all your available information on restaurants, but then the information in the story started to conflict with your existing knowledge—galleries, songs, applause, etc. At that point in the story, you either gave up or you worked even harder to make sense of what you were reading by explaining away the contradictory information. Maybe "Jim" was a famous singer and his song was playing on the sound system in the restaurant; that would also explain the applause. But "proceeding with the preparation"? Now we are stuck again!

The point here is to show you how much effort is involved in the comprehension process. The authors of this story invented a restaurant where the customers compete for the right to cook their favorite dish. If they win the loudest applause, they can go to the kitchen and prepare a dish to serve to the customers in the restaurant. If they earn enough money, then they can buy a meal for themselves and keep the extra money that they earned. This is all quite absurd, I know, but again, the point of this story is to demonstrate to you how hard you work when you are reading and how much additional information you bring with you to a text.

Work Those Schemas

The background knowledge that children (and adults) must access as they read is stored in "schemas."[66] When children learn new, meaningful knowledge, they store it. If you go to a birthday party, you know what to expect. You know because you access your birthday party schema—everything you know on the topic stored in your memory. This schema, or integrated neural network of knowledge, beliefs, and expectations, helps you to fill in gaps and make inferences. For example, if I asked you to go to McDonald's and get me a ". . ." (fill in the blank), I am relatively confident that you can fill in the blank based on your schematic knowledge of fast food.

Go to McDonald's and get me a...

You would also know immediately that something was wrong if I asked you to "go to McDonald's and get me a pizza." You would know this because your McDonald's schema doesn't contain pizzas. Your schematic knowledge tells you that McDonald's does not sell pizza! These schemata form the very foundation of our knowledge. They are an essential component of the reading process.

Why Rabbits Sometimes Eat Spilled Pizza

Ideas are connected to one another both within and among schemas. The current thinking is that neural networks connect this information using the parallel distributed processing approach, or the "PDP" model.[67] The idea is that nodes in our neural network become activated by the environment. The neural pathway that is followed from that point is determined by the strength of any given connection. This neural network could operate at any level—it could be a concept, a word, or a letter—but the same principle applies: the stronger the connection, the more likely the activation. It is called "parallel" because the search that occurs happens in parallel, or at the same time, within this integrated neural network.

If I asked a group of 4-year-olds the question "what do rabbits eat?," their potential neural search could look something like the fictitious neural network in Box 9 below. "Rabbits" activates many different types of animals, and "eat" activates the types of activities that animals engage in. This opens up a whole realm of possible foods, but "vegetables" receives the greatest strength. This will make a great deal more sense if you follow along with Box 9. In this fictitious example, the color of the vegetable is activated next, but any attribute could have followed. The neural network ends in "carrot" and our 4-year-olds blurt out "carrots," en masse.

This works well in our neat little example, but children have varying schema and neural networks since they are built based on knowledge and interaction with the environment. Sometimes when you ask a question like "what do rabbits eat?," you can get some really off base responses. Say, for instance, a child bursts into tears and says something like "I spilled my pizza on the carpet!" How does the PDP model account for that? Look at Box 9 below and see if you can follow that child's connections. In this hypothetical example, eating led to a connection with the time of day, not types of food. This led to lunch, which activated pizza (maybe she had pizza for lunch), which led to a recollection of spilling her lunch all over the carpet.

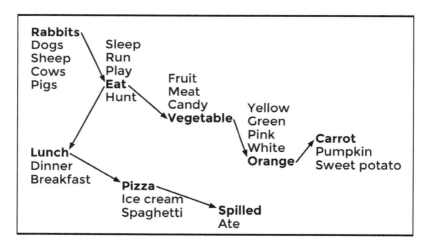

Box 9 PDP Model—Integrated Neural Network

Maybe Men Aren't from Mars After All

This also explains why, in the midst of a conversation, your spouse may suddenly add information that may seem irrelevant to you. This is precisely because your spouse's neural network may have veered off in a different direction from yours (perish the thought).

Stick to the Script

Information within our schemas appears to be organized in "scripts." A script, like the script in a play, allows a child as young as 3 years of age to predict what will happen or how an event might unfold.[68] Children often rigidly adhere to these scripts. Take, for example, a kindergarten class whose teacher is out for the day. The substitute teacher who tries to read a story after "circle time" when the routine clearly calls for "snack time" will find that violating the children's scripts can lead to chaos! Adults are meant to be more flexible (maybe Mars is looking more likely again).

Scripting Childhood

Now that we know children store knowledge in schemas that contain detailed scripts, it is our job as parents and educators to tap into those preexisting schema and scripts so that we can help children build on their preexisting knowledge when they read. When children link new ideas to an existing schema, it is helpful in 2 ways. First, the thought is connected to a body of knowledge, therefore it is less likely to be a random fact. This, in turn, may lead to a deeper level of processing and the ability to connect new ideas to known or existing knowledge. One of the key differences between novices and experts is the ability to think deeply about a concept and to link ideas. We are, in essence, discussing the organization of our memory system, which is a vital part of the reading process.

I Never Thought of That

There are so many ways that we can enhance children's reading based on this model. Have you ever, for example, taken a test and thought that you had done really well, until you saw your grade? You thought that you gave the correct answers. When you saw the answers that the teacher was looking for, you recognized them but didn't think to link that particular question to that particular response. Using a child-centered approach—where we try to tap into a child's existing neural network—encourages the likelihood that the right connections will be made. This allows the child to utilize existing knowledge to process new information. This allows the child to link the knowledge to other relevant information. Keeping to "child-friendly" topics might include stories about the park, the zoo, helping out at home, trees, or other topics that children might have experience with.

Necessary Knowledge

Thinking again about novice readers, imagine a first- or second-grade child trying to comprehend a story about the Aztecs or working in a coal mine. Without the necessary background information, a story can be extremely hard to comprehend. We need, therefore, to make sure that our readers have schematic knowledge to bring with them to a text in order to maximize their comprehension success. Children rely on scripts, not only in reading, but to compensate for their limited cognitive capacity and experience in life.[69] Scripts allow children to navigate their day by relying on what they know.

Given the developmental and cognitive limitations of our children and their scripts and schemas, it seems imperative that we focus on those limitations during the reading process. It seems odd to this cognitive psychologist that something this important wouldn't receive at least the same attention as decoding!

These background knowledge limitations have implications for the teaching process. We must modify our expectations of novice readers who are trying to learn new information on an unfamiliar topic presented in a text. In the earlier grades, we ought to present children with passages that they can relate to and we ought to discuss the subject matter in advance to allow for success.

When children fail at reading, and many do, it ought not to be because they lacked the necessary background knowledge. Similarly, at what age do we ask a child to read a chapter of a social studies textbook or a science textbook and expect them to learn new knowledge? At what age should we expect that level of comprehension?

MYTH:
"Academic programs that focus on learning
the ABCs and reading short words are more
valuable than programs that focus on play"

MYTH BUSTED:
Academic programs that focus on learning the
ABCs and reading short words are not more
valuable than programs that focus on play,
as they have the potential to short-change
our children in the long run . . .

Some parents mistakenly believe that their preschoolers'
time is well spent on ditto sheets or formal instruction to
achieve literacy through decoding success. If children are to
bring background knowledge with them to a story, then they
must first acquire that knowledge. If the story is about a girl
who loves to jump in puddles, then think of the wealth of
knowledge that children will develop about this subject if they
are well versed in puddle jumping. Think of how much more
meaningful the story will be and how much more children
can appreciate the themes within that story. This underscores
the critical importance of pretend play, field trips, and life
experience.

This problem is compounded for many parents who pay for child care. They want their money's worth (and rightly so). They want to hear their children reciting the alphabet, and they want to see their children reading simple words. How can we persuade these parents that play and field trips contribute to the vital background knowledge that will turn children into lifelong readers?

CHAPTER 14

IN WHICH WE MOVE FROM MYTHS (AND THEIR BUSTING) TO NEW KNOWLEDGE . . .

It's Just Not That Simple

I f only it were really this straightforward: give them background knowledge and "boom," you've solved the reading problem for thousands of children. Unfortunately, there is more to the comprehension/background knowledge saga. To give you an idea of what less skilled readers experience, read Box 10 below. Before you read it, get a pencil and put it beside you.

The procedure is actually quite simple. First you arrange items into different groups. Of course, one pile may be sufficient depending on how much there is to do. If you have to go somewhere else due to lack of facilities, that is the next step; otherwise, you are pretty well set. It is important to not overdo things. That is, it is better to do a few things at once than too many. In the short run, this may not seem important but complications can easily arise. A mistake can be expensive as well. At first, the whole procedure will seem complicated. Soon, however, it will become just another facet of life. It is difficult to foresee any end to the necessity for this task in the immediate future, but then, one never can tell . . .

(Bransford & Johnson, 1972)

Box 10

Now, having read Box 10 and before you read the contents of Box 11, take the pencil that you so diligently put by your side and write down everything that you can remember, or you can just close your eyes and try to recall as much as you can:

_____

_____

_____

_____

_____

_____

_____

_____

_____

_____

_____

_____

Not much going on, right? Now read Box 11 on the following page.

The Washing Clothes Passage

The procedure is actually quite simple. First you arrange items into different groups. Of course, one pile may be sufficient depending on how much there is to do. If you have to go somewhere else due to lack of facilities, that is the next step; otherwise, you are pretty well set. It is important to not overdo things. That is, it is better to do a few things at once than too many. In the short run, this may not seem important but complications can easily arise. A mistake can be expensive as well. At first, the whole procedure will seem complicated. Soon, however, it will become just another facet of life. It is difficult to foresee any end to the necessity for this task in the immediate future, but then, one never can tell . . .

Bransford & Johnson, 1972

Box 11

It was the same passage, so why was Box 11 so much easier to follow? It wasn't because you read it for a second time (if you don't believe me then find an unsuspecting spouse or friend and get him or her to read only Box 10 twice then ask the unsuspecting spouse or friend to write down what he or she can remember!). Easier yet, just take my word for it—it wasn't the second reading! Look again at Box 11, at the top. It has a title! The only difference between Boxes 10 and 11 is the title in Box 11. You knew all about doing the laundry when you read Box 10 but you probably didn't think to apply that knowledge to the text. When you read the title on Box 11, you automatically accessed your schematic knowledge of laundry and applied it to the text. It was probably effortless and made the passage much easier to read than Box 10.

Apply as Needed

How does this apply to our children? Teaching them to read the title is imperative. It accesses their schematic knowledge and allows them to bring background knowledge with them to the text. This example also demonstrates how much work we do when we read. It is not sufficient to say the words out loud—we know that—but here is a magnificent demonstration of how much work we do beyond simply decoding. Skilled readers naturally do all of this additional work, but we need to teach our less skilled readers to do the same.

Again, this laundry passage emphasizes the idea that we may have the relevant information stored in our brains but we don't always know that we should apply it. We should stress the importance of the title when we read with our children and we should encourage them to talk about the themes, events, and locations of the stories that they are reading about. Teaching children to use the title is vital to the comprehension process.

It is time to move beyond our unnatural focus on decoding fluency to enjoy proposition integration, schematic knowledge, and schematic access as precursors to formal reading instruction. These are key components of the reading process that can be nurtured in the preschool years and developed in the primary grades.

CHAPTER 15

LET'S AGREE TO DISAGREE . . .

Cognitive developmental research has revealed the importance of what takes place in the minutes before a child reads. Read the story in Box 12 and imagine you are a real estate agent. I promise it won't violate your schematic knowledge and it has a title for easy schematic access: "The House Passage"! So imagine you are a real estate agent and read on . . .

The House Passage

The 2 boys ran until they came to the driveway. "See, I told you today was good for skipping school," said Mark. "Mom is never home on Thursday," he added. Tall hedges hid the house from the road so the pair strolled across the finely landscaped yard. "I never knew your place was so big," said Pete. "Yeah, but it's nicer now than it used to be since Dad had the new stone siding put on and added that fireplace."

There were front and back doors and a side door which led to the garage, which was empty except for 3 parked 10-speed bikes. They went in the side door, Mark explaining that it was always open in case his younger sisters got home earlier than their mother.

Pete wanted to see the house so Mark started with the living room. It, like the rest of the downstairs, was newly painted. Mark turned on the stereo, the noise of which worried Pete. "Don't worry, the nearest house is a quarter of a mile away," Mark shouted. Pete felt more comfortable observing that no houses could be seen in any direction beyond the huge yard.

The dining room, with all the china, silver, and cut glass, was no place to play so the boys moved into the kitchen, where they made sandwiches. Mark said they wouldn't go to the basement because it had been damp and musty ever since the new plumbing had been installed. "This is where my dad keeps his famous paintings and his coin collection," Mark said as they peered into a den. Mark bragged that he could get spending money whenever he needed it since he'd discovered that his dad kept a lot in the desk drawer.

There were 3 upstairs bedrooms. Mark showed Pete his mother's closet, which was filled with furs, and the locked box which held her jewels. His sisters' room was uninteresting except for the color TV, which Mark carried to his room. Mark bragged that the bathroom in the hall was his since one had been added to his sisters' room for their use. The big highlight in his room, though, was the leak in the ceiling where the old roof had finally rotted.

(Pichert & Anderson, 1977)

Box 12—The House Passage

Now see if you can answer the following questions (without looking back at the story):

- How many bedrooms were there in the house?
- Was there privacy from other homes?
- What had been recently updated in the home?
- What problems did the house have?

Now try these questions:

- Which day would the mother not be home?
- What was in the garage?
- Could you get into the house if you wanted to sneak in without a key?
- In which room in the house could the son find money if he wanted it?
- Where did the mother keep her jewels?

Which questions were easier to answer?

You ought to have found that the first set of questions were easier. It turns out that the perspective that you bring to a passage can influence your interpretation and recall.[70] Now reread the story as if you were a "burglar casing the joint" and see if your perspective makes a difference.

State of Mind

This once again highlights the importance of what a reader brings to a text. The reader's perspective obviously plays a key role in the interpretation and recall of a story. It is also surprising that the state of mind you're in when you read a text can have such a profound effect on your recall and comprehension.

Act on It

If point of view is so essential to comprehension, then think of how beneficial acting out stories can be for children. Think about how much insight even high school students could glean from a text if they actually played the part of a character in a story. Better yet, think of what a wonderful "cognitive crutch" this is for less skilled readers. Imagine being Juliet and waking up to discover your poisoned Romeo by your side.[71] Which child wouldn't feel Jane Eyre's shame and humiliation if she were to stand on a stool in the middle of her classroom and hear Mr. Brocklehurst's cruel character assault[72]? While this doesn't have to be a full-scale production, acting out age-appropriate scenes in the classroom can be a powerful comprehension tool. Yet again, this helps less skilled readers of any age turn the covert process of reading comprehension into a more overt, or observable, activity. Acting out scenes also reduces the cognitive load for less skilled readers so that they can focus on the meaning of the text, giving them more opportunity to explore the thoughts, motives, or implications of a character's actions.

CHAPTER 16

WHO IS LETTING THE TEAM DOWN?

In this high-stakes testing environment that has become our educational norm, who is scoring poorly on those reading comprehension tests? It's tempting to blame the "bad" readers for poor test scores in a group, isn't it? After all, not all children are skilled readers. To figure out who is letting the proverbial team down, let's further divide the third- and sixth-grade children into skilled and less skilled readers. It stands to reason that less skilled readers ought to have more difficulty with reading comprehension tasks than their skilled counterparts.[73] Let's revisit the results based on the skilled versus less skilled reader distinction.

Looking first at the third-grade group, we were right! Only 13% of the less skilled readers noticed problems in stories versus 46% of the more skilled readers. In sixth grade, however, the difference was much smaller: 38% of the less skilled readers noticed the problem versus 50% of the skilled readers. If you prefer to read tables, I have printed these statistics in Table 1.

	Less Skilled Readers	Skilled Readers
Third Grade	13%	46%
Sixth Grade	38%	50%

Table 1 –Inconsistency Detection Rates in Third- and Sixth-Grade Students (Rubman & Waters, 2000)

Do as They Do—But Better

To summarize, we have clearly demonstrated that some children have reading comprehension problems. We have ascertained that skilled readers perform better than their less skilled counterparts. To address this issue then, let's focus on what skilled readers do that less skilled readers apparently fail to do.

Imagine That!

The comprehension monitoring abilities of skilled readers have been assessed and analyzed.[74] It appears that skilled readers form a mental representation of the text that allows them to build on an idea, store multiple facts, or notice inconsistent information. Less skilled readers don't seem to form this mental representation. Instead, they attend to smaller portions of a text, engaging in "piecemeal processing."[75] Less skilled readers fail to successfully integrate idea units or propositions across the length of a story.

This piecemeal processing certainly accounts for fish jumping in and out of frozen ponds while children ice skate on water.

When children attend simply to the meaning of individual phrases and sentences rather than the comprehensibility of an entire story, the meaning can become seriously distorted. The stories that they read, if you recall, were very simple narratives—the story about Tim, Lisa, and Tiddles the cat, for example. Imagine what these third and sixth graders might do with the French Revolution or the life story of Mahatma Gandhi.

Actively Non-Planful

To further compound this problem, children's thinking in general has been characterized as passive, non-strategic, and non-planful.[76] This doesn't bode well for a reading process that appears to require the active building of some type of mental image involving an interactive process. It seems that many of our youngsters are sitting waiting for books to read themselves.

We Need a Non-Strategic Strategy

How can we encourage more interactivity between our children and their stories? We can certainly focus on using texts with more familiar settings. We can continue to work on enhancing our children's schematic knowledge (as we did in the earlier grades), but is that enough?

Board with Reading

Here's a suggestion that comes straight from the developmental literature. Now that we have identified the processes that skilled readers utilize when comprehending a text (they build mental models of the story as they read, remember), let's simulate that process for our less skilled population. Let's train our less skilled readers to integrate propositions by building dynamic mental representations of the text that they are reading.

To do this we need to externalize the processes of proposition assembly and proposition integration for less skilled readers so that they can learn how to simulate the process that their skilled counterparts use naturally. In other words, we need to teach less skilled readers to build a visual image or representation of what they are reading. To encourage this process, we need to use an overt (visual) process instead of the covert (internalized) process that skilled readers naturally use.

Making the Covert—Overt

This can be done by using "storyboards." Storyboards have been shown to aid comprehension by providing a visual and tactile crutch that externalizes a previously covert, or hidden, process. Storyboards teach less skilled readers what they should be doing when they attempt to comprehend. Constructing the storyboard teaches children to use the same process of reading comprehension that their skilled counterparts use naturally.

Storyboards make a previously covert process more overt and easier to fathom. Storyboards can make proposition assembly and integration more tangible.

Now Children, Take Out Your Imaginations . . .

Why, I hear you ask, would this really help? Isn't it tantamount to giving them a picture book or a video of the story, and isn't that also a form of cheating? Why no, actually, the storyboard serves a different purpose. The difference between the board and a premade picture is the amount of input from the reader. It is the interactive nature of the storyboard that creates the difference. Building a mental model outside of your imagination alleviates the cognitive overload that may have hampered comprehension success in the past. It avoids the necessity for children to split their available cognitive resources between visualizing a textual proposition, holding it in working memory, and, subsequently, integrating it with other idea units.[77]

Below you will see the corresponding storyboard for "The Snowy Day" story described earlier. A child would read each sentence of the story and apply the magnetic cutout figures accordingly. As the story reaches its conclusion, the child would build an externalized representation of the mental model that a skilled reader builds so effortlessly.

A Snowy Day

It had been snowing all afternoon, but it was not yet cold enough for the pond at the bottom of the yard to freeze over with ice. Tiddles the cat sat by the front door patiently waiting for someone to let her back into the warm house. She had been outside all afternoon watching the children, Tim and Lisa, playing in the snow. The children had wanted to skate on the fishpond, but since it was not cold enough for the pond to freeze, they had built a snowman instead. They were delighted with their snowman that now stood beside the old pine tree. Having finished their snowman, the children were now skating happily across the fishpond while the fish jumped in and out of the water. Tiddles looked at the fish and dreamed of dinner.

(Rubman & Waters, 2000)

Mind Reading

The storyboards work! They helped the less skilled third-grade children achieve a dramatic 41% improvement in inconsistency detection rates. They even helped the skilled readers, whose inconsistency detection rates rose to 67%.

The same holds true for sixth-grade readers who all benefited from the externalized, tactile crutch. This clearly demonstrates that when children engage in a more interactive, hands-on approach to learning, their comprehension rates increase. The message is loud and clear: Don't just sit there; use that mind and actively process while you read!

Table 2 shows the inconsistency detection rates with and without the storyboard construction.

	Third Grade Less Skilled	Third Grade Skilled	Sixth Grade Less Skilled	Sixth Grade Skilled
% improvement	41%	21%	29%	21%
Read only	13%	46%	38%	50%
Read & Construct Storyboard	54%	67%	67%	71%

Table 2 Inconsistency Detection Rates with and without the Storyboard Construction.

Resuscitating Reading

How, then, can we encourage more children to interact with the text and with greater frequency? It is time that we made reading much more of an interactive process. It is time that we had more fun with reading and challenged our children to think. Many of our great teachers already inspire our children to think. While they do it very successfully, there are many that don't.

Oh, the Lies We've Told

Instead of focusing on a reading program, teaching to the test, or following a specific set of textbooks, let's go back to basics. Classic children's literature is so exciting; for example, should Anne Shirley forgive Gilbert Blythe in *Anne of Green Gables*? What did Gilbert do that was so terrible? This should lead to a discussion about making poor choices and asking friends to forgive you, or even a discussion on the concept of forgiveness. Under what circumstances would it be acceptable to invent a "Great Aunt Bertha" if you never had one, like in *Number the Stars*? A discussion about when it's acceptable to lie ought to motivate children to want to read on, or at least to take a deeper look at the text. What about a lesson that motivates a group of 12-year-olds to turn a chore into a highly coveted activity to parallel how Tom managed to change the mindset of his entire peer group and turn painting the fence into the fun activity of the day in *The Adventures of Tom Sawyer*?

Comprehending Fun

These are fun, interesting, and relevant questions that come from classic children's literature. Let's bring reading back to life in the classroom and turn it from a chore into a fun, interactive, constructive process—even among our kindergarten and preschool populations. Reading circles and reading detectives are a great step in the right direction because they assign different tasks to different children. Within a certain chapter, one student might look up difficult vocabulary words, one might work on characters, yet another (the director) could discuss the plot.

Let's get our children up out of their seats and acting out these stories, which will give them more meaning and bring their words to life! Remember, it will also help them approach the text from a new perspective. Let's read the stories in small groups so that the less skilled readers can focus on listening instead of decoding. Let's teach our children to read with expression in their voices. Children need this understanding if, later on in their educational journey, they are to care about why Lady Macbeth must wash her hands so obsessively or why the Capulets hate the Montagues in *Romeo and Juliet*. Our children watch hours of television, so they obviously enjoy a good story just like the rest of us. How can we motivate them to read with as much passion as they have for watching television?

Stop Teaching So Much

De-emphasizing decoding is just the first step! Teaching our children to integrate propositions and form active mental images is crucial too, but the environment in which we discuss these stories is also of paramount importance. Children need to feel comfortable in an environment where they can explore their background knowledge and their newly forming neural networks. It isn't always easy to maintain that risk-free environment. Yet, asking children to express their opinion or debate contentious issues demands that we guarantee them that sense of non-judgmental safety.

Our goal here is to create a learning environment like the environment that exists around the family dinner table. This is where we can see evidence of a frank exchange of ideas in a risk-free, non-judgmental environment. Compare this to the standardized and clinical setting of formal education where much of the learning is rote memorization and there is sometimes little room for debate, creativity, and true understanding. We need to de-emphasize rote responses and testing in favor of a deeper level of understanding. In deference to this, we need to stop teaching to the test because it is getting in the way of a higher level of learning.

CHAPTER 17

JUST TEACH THEM TO READ (WE'LL DO THE REST LATER)

Idealistic Hype

All this talk of de-emphasizing phonics and focusing on meaning is all fine and well if you've made it through school and have safely arrived in adulthood. If, however, you are trapped within the American educational system in the 21st century and you're just trying to get to fourth grade, without the help of social promotion, then maybe you need to rethink all that idealistic "hype" and stick to decoding and rote memorization. Let's be honest, do standardized tests really care whether you chose answer "a" because you passionately believed in the underlying truth behind it? Or, more realistically, is it just one more incorrect response because it says so on page 97 of your textbook? If we want our children to shine in kindergarten, shouldn't we just teach them to decode and worry about all those minor comprehension details later? If we want our children to be placed in honors classes, shouldn't we give them a jump-start and focus on reading early? After all, they have to excel on all of those state-mandated tests . . .

Testing Them Silly

We have ELAs, Tera Novas, Regents, SATs, PSATs, SSATs, ACTs, and state math and science exams. Frankly, we are a nation that has become plagued by tests. The "No Child Left Behind Act" has ensured that we have tested our children silly, if you will, for the last several years. We have been inundated with these tests in an attempt to improve the quality of learning in our public schools. All we've really succeeded in doing, however, is teaching our children how to take tests—and not very well, apparently, since 70% of fourth-grade inner-city children can't even read at the basic level. Remember, 40–60% of all college freshmen took remedial reading classes in 2018.[78] Ironically, the "NCLB Act," this "blueprint for educational reform," was designed to ensure that "every child should be educated to his or her full potential."[79]

Just Look What We Left Behind!

Long before the "No Child Left Behind Act," our government was hard at work addressing this academic epidemic by spending $120 billion per year on programs and tests for children. Whoa! 120,000,000,000 dollars . . . that sounds like a lot of money to me. Since so many of our nation's children were failing to maintain even a minimal standard in 2001, clearly money wasn't the answer here!

Illiteracy, or to use its politically correct term "the reading deficit," has been addressed by the "Reading First Initiative," a key component of the "No Child Left Behind Act."[80] This initiative was devised by a government-appointed panel who reviewed 100,000 studies on reading and how students learn. In an official "foreword" issued by the White House, this is what that panel of experts learned from their 100,000 studies:

"Effective reading instruction includes teaching children to break apart and manipulate the sounds in words (phonemic awareness), teaching them that these sounds are represented by letters of the alphabet which can then be blended together to form words (phonics), having them practice what they have learned by reading aloud with guidance and feedback (guided oral reading), and applying reading comprehension strategies to guide and improve reading comprehension."

Really . . . 100,000 studies and that's all they got?

The Reading Deficit

Oh wait, they've got money too: "The Reading First initiative gives states both the funds and the tools they need to eliminate the reading deficit." Gosh, "reading deficit" makes it sound like part of our national debt! Does our government really believe that we can throw money at the problem and expect it to go away? Didn't we just establish that $120 billion a year couldn't solve the nation's illiteracy pre-2001? How much has been spent since 2001? How much more are we planning to spend on this so-called reading deficit? If you read the details of this "NCLB" Act, there's a section on "Rewarding Success and Sanctioning Failure" for you to consider:

Excerpt from the No Child Left Behind (NCLB) Act

Rewarding Success and Sanctioning Failure:

Rewards for Closing the Achievement Gap: High performing states that narrow the achievement gap and improve overall student achievement will be rewarded.

Accountability Bonus for States: Each state will be offered a one-time bonus if it meets accountability requirements, including establishing annual assessments in grades 3-8, within 2 years of enacting this plan.

"No Child Left Behind" School Rewards: Successful schools that have made the greatest progress in improving the achievement of disadvantaged students will be recognized and rewarded with "No Child Left Behind" bonuses.

Consequences for Failure: The Secretary of Education will be authorized to reduce federal funds available to a state for administrative expenses if a state fails to meet their performance objectives and demonstrate results in academic achievement.

(Excerpt from the No Child Left Behind Act, 2001)

How can we allow our children's education to be treated like a business? How can we allow the risk-free environment that learning demands to be threatened by financial bonuses and monetary penalties for schools? Congress, what is going on? Our children are not for sale. "Accountability bonuses," "NCLB School rewards" who on Capitol Hill endorsed this plan?

If It's Broke—Fix It

It is a noble goal to have all of our nation's third graders reading competently; I'm sure no one would dispute that. Then there's the "Reading Excellence Act"—another great idea! It is also wonderful that our government wants to promote early literacy. Pre-reading skills can certainly be encouraged among our young children. We must, however, review this information from a cognitive developmental perspective:

- Teaching the names of the letters is not the most productive use of a 3-, 4-, or even 5-year-old's time.

- Superficial strategies that teach children to pronounce words on a page without focusing on the deeper underlying comprehension will result in short-term gains. These superficial skills often backfire on our children when they try to comprehend meaningful texts, chapters, and books as they progress through the higher grades.

- Decoding is important in reading, but comprehension skills need to be taught and practiced simultaneously. We need to teach our children how to understand what they read.

- Flash cards don't teach children to read; they frustrate children who lack the experience to recognize words like adults can. We read within a context: There is a story, surrounding words, and there are often pictures. Flash cards remove all the contextual clues that we want to encourage children to use.

- In an attempt to encourage their children to read, parents try to switch from reading to their children to having their children read to them. Encouraging children to sound out stories can be a frustrating experience for children, which can ultimately put them off reading, and delay or even prevent them from ever discovering the experience of a really great book. We have established that young children lack the cognitive capacity to sound out letters, form words, and still have enough cognitive resources to follow a story.

Money Doesn't Teach Children to Read

Let's review:

- Throwing billions of dollars at our nation's children hasn't improved their reading scores, so money doesn't seem to help children learn to read.

- Paying schools to narrow the gap between the achievers and the non-achievers hasn't improved their test scores, so financial incentives haven't taught our children to read.

- Threatening consequences, like taking away government funding for schools that don't perform well on state tests, hasn't improved those reading skills, so taking money away hasn't taught our children to read.

Would it be fair, at this point, to conclude that there seems to be very little correlation between reading scores and money?

What's next for our illiterate friends? What does the government have in mind? Extrinsic financial rewards and punishments aside, is there a plan?

Oh, Oh I Know

Dare I propose that we reinvent learning? Let's intrinsically motivate our children to read and learn by making reading fun, instead of how we find an answer on a multiple-choice comprehension test. Let's read exciting stories instead of focusing on drill and practice so that we don't lose our funding. Let's give reading a purpose. We could read recipes while we cook, follow directions on class trips, and read movie reviews to plan social events. We could read emails and instant messages. We could play fun, interactive games on the computer, and, if all else fails, we could always resort to books.

Oh, and let's not forget comprehension for our pre-readers. Let's actually teach children how to comprehend. We can teach the importance of a title, background knowledge, schematic access, a picture, an integrated set of propositions, or your perspective as you read a story.

We could act out stories so that children can follow the plot and character development. We can learn to build mental models of the story and follow the storyline in our heads. We could predict endings and we could imagine the possibilities.

There are so many excellent teachers in our classrooms already doing so much more than these basic suggestions for our children. They are professionals after all; they know how to teach. They don't need pressure from their local school districts to get good test scores. What they need is their academic freedom in the classroom. They need their creativity back, and that will only happen when the pressure to constantly test our children is removed. We don't need a national curriculum. We don't need all fourth or eighth graders to know the same rote facts so that they can become a statistic in the next government report. We need to take a closer look at what it means to teach a child.

Giving Information

Teaching a child is not about giving that child information. It is about following a child's train of thought to seek out ideas. Teaching means that we support a child's effort to discover what we adults all too often already know, instead of telling a child the answer. Teaching involves guiding a young mind, encouraging creativity, and nurturing interest. Children are naturally curious, and that curiosity should fuel each school day. Clearly there must be order in the classroom, but within the framework of a science topic or a math concept, there must be room for individual thought. Each child is as unique as his or her neural network. We should embrace that diversity. Teaching involves the creation of dynamic situations for exploration. Teaching is the ability to inspire our children to think, question, and reason.

Cheap Approximations

Telling a child information is not teaching. It is a superficial, shallow means to accomplish a testable goal. Standardized, multiple-choice tests do not tap into the wealth of knowledge that a student could potentially learn during any school semester. They are a cheap approximation of a child's abilities. They are the antithesis of true assessment. True assessment would measure learning outcomes that have been clearly established by a viable set of learning objectives. They can be detailed in a grading rubric that clearly delineates success and accomplishment from inactivity and stagnation. This type of measure is adaptable to different situations and learning styles. It cannot be drilled or practiced. It recognizes where a student's learning began and taps into individual progress. It values the process of learning and is not fixated on the learned product.

Pressure in Preschool

Reading is the linchpin of all future learning. In principle, while we should focus on reading as early as possible, we shouldn't follow the current trend to formally instruct children or to teach letters and decoding skills to 3-, 4-, and 5-year-olds. At this tender age, children are developing at a staggering rate. We, however, are not privy to that process. We should, therefore, rely on our children's verbal cues and behavior. Much like toilet training, they'll let us know when they are ready. In the interim, let's set the stage for them. Let's build solid educational foundations with our children. Listening comprehension and reading comprehension share many of the same basic foundations. Let's use listening skills to teach many of the basic skills that are also required for reading. Let's teach our children to think and to actively process information. Let's reinvent "pre-reading" skills to actually correspond to age-appropriate activities that are fun, motivational, and will ultimately lead to lifelong readers who choose to read and will one day be able to enjoy a good book.

Do Children Actually Choose to Read?

In this fast-paced, high-tech world that we live in, do our children actually choose to read? Let's say we try a giant social experiment:

What if we were all locked in our respective homes and we couldn't really go out or interact with others for, say . . . March through May (say . . . in the year 2020). Would our children read? Would they actually choose to read books, given that they'd have all that free time . . .

Let's fast-forward to the present day, to our post Covid-19 pandemic era and take a closer look at the results of our giant social experiment (that obviously actually happened). Did our children read more? Did their reading improve?

Well, sorry to say, reading scores actually declined for 9-year-olds across the United States of America. The average child dropped 5 points in 2022 reading exams according to the "National Report Card" by the National Assessment of Educational Progress.[81] Children who were classified as "weaker readers" lost up to 10 points, while readers in the 90th percentile lost around 2 points.

This precipitous drop in reading scores appears to be the greatest decline in any assessment period in the entire 50 years that the NAEP program has assessed students.

These lower scores were due to "a lack of in-person classroom education during the Covid-19 pandemic" according to the US

Secretary of Education, Miguel Cardona.[82] What did Miguel believe was happening in the classroom that did not happen in a child's home? Indeed, what was not happening in many 9-year-olds' homes across the country?

Similarly, scores for the graduating class of 2022 showed declines in reading skills across the nation. This continues a downward trend in "ACT" reading test scores for the last 4 consecutive years culminating in more than 40% of graduating high school seniors who did not meet the benchmark reading comprehension requirements. These benchmarks predict college success.[83] [84]

But Why?

Why didn't the pandemic afford our children the time they needed to read vociferously and raise their "reading scores" though the proverbial roof? Why isn't reading the national pastime of choice for our nation's children?

CHAPTER 18

THE BRAINS BEHIND THE PLAN

In order to truly appreciate how children learn to read and process information, we need a clear understanding of how they think and remember. Let's look at where information goes and how it is stored. Answer the questions in the boxes below and then we'll discuss the answers.

Take the Test:

Word Recall Task

Instructions:

Look at the words below for exactly 30 seconds. At the end of 30 seconds go to the next page and write down as many as you can remember. Go.

hut	chisel	hotel
cliff	hill	volcano
ant	wasp	mosquito
river	saw	nail
drill	tent	
cottage	beetle	

Box 12 Word Recall Task[85]

Fill In Your Answers to the Following Questions:

1. From the previous page, see how many you can write in the spaces below:

_____   _____
_____   _____
_____   _____
_____   _____
_____   _____
_____   _____
_____   _____
_____   _____

2. Draw a penny in the space below:

3. Write the name of your kindergarten teacher:

_____

4. What is the capital of Scotland?

_____

Now think about the following concepts: Why was it so difficult to draw a penny if you use one every day? How could your kindergarten teacher's name be so readily available given that you didn't exactly attend kindergarten yesterday? Did you know the capital in #4? If not, think about how you knew that you didn't know! If you did know, how did you find that information? We know a great deal about the function of human memory. First, we'll look at the research on adult memory, and then we'll discuss children.

Let's start with Question #1:

How Much Is Normal?

Question #1 required you to recall a list of words. How did you fare? How many words did you recall? How many should you have been able to recall? There were 16 words in all. The human memory can recall between 5 and 9 units, or chunks of information, in a task like this one. This is known as "The Magic Number 7 plus or minus 2,"[86] since that's the capacity of your short-term memory system. If you want to recall information for a limited amount of time, then this is the storage system to use! Be warned, however, that information falls out of short-term memory within 15–30 seconds!

The Magic Number 7 + or - 2

Box 13 The Capacity of Short-Term Memory [87]

What about those of you who recalled more than 9 items? Are you our resident geniuses, our gifted and talented readers? It is not simply a question of filling up 9 words in your short-term memory store, or "STM," because capacity is dependent on your organizational strategies. We have "slots" in our STM and recall capacity depends on how we utilize those slots. You may have noticed that there were 4 categories within that word list, including dwellings, land formations, bugs, and tools. You could have encoded the information using those categories or, as competent adults, you could have used any number of other strategies. Perhaps you repeated the words over and over—that's called rehearsal.[88] Perhaps you made up a story or linked the words in a meaningful way—that's called elaboration![89] Whatever strategy you use, you maximized your short-term memory capacity. Well done!

How many words should you remember? Are we bound by that magic number 7 plus or minus 2? As a rough guide for your memory span, you ought to be able to remember as many words as you can rehearse in 2 seconds (which usually turns out to be 7 plus or minus 2!). There is another common strategy for maximizing our memory span called "chunking." Try recalling the letters below:

INTELIBMNASAFDA

They become much easier to recall if you chunk them into more meaningful units:

INTEL
IBM
NASA
FDA

Your bank and your phone company, not to mention the federal government, have known this information for years. What is your social security number? How did you recite it? Was it XXX then XX followed by XXXX? Chunking, right? We know that 9 digits are tricky to remember, so your kindly neighborhood government chunked the numbers for you, knowing that 3 chunks are more likely to be recalled than 9 straight digits.

Check your phone number—1 (XXX) area code, followed by XXX then XXXX. 11 digits, 2 too many for the average working memory! Once again, your friendly neighborhood phone company chunked the numbers because 3 chunks are better than 11 digits.

Your bank account number? Not so chunked! Do you know your bank account number? How about the "routing" number? Too many digits, eh? Compare that with your credit card number—that one you know, right? You can claim it's because you use it to buy stuff online, but be honest with yourself—it's because it's chunked and ready for recall!

What Can Children Remember?

90

Children's Limits

What about children? They don't have bank accounts, but do they utilize chunking, rehearsal, and elaboration strategies for short-term memory? Is the short-term memory capacity of a child equal to that of an adult? The truth is, we can't actually measure the structure itself, so we don't really know if the place that we call memory grows in physical size like a hand or a foot grows. However, we do know that the utilization of that capacity increases with age.

As you might expect, an adult can recall more from STM than a 10-year-old who, in turn, can recall more than a 4-year-old.[91] STM, or working memory as it is also known, is better utilized as children age. Older children can rehearse more words in a shorter time period, they can elaborate on ideas, and they can chunk more meaningfully than younger children. Each of these improvements in strategy leads to more efficiency in working memory.

A Penny for Your Thoughts

How did you do with Question #2? Could you draw a penny replete with all its details? If not, why couldn't you draw a penny?

Can you, at least, recognize a penny? Look at the 10 pennies below; which one is the real penny?

Box 14 Which One is The Real Penny? [92]

The answer lies in what we call "encoding failures." We encode information that is essential or useful to us; the rest we ignore! I'm sure you could differentiate between a dime and a penny, but the actual details of a penny are not essential so we simply don't encode them. We call this encoding failure.[93] It is not that you stored the information and have forgotten it; the reality is that you never paid attention to the details in the first place. That said, you know when you end up with a Canadian penny. Luckily our brain is cognitively efficient. Since we can't possibly remember everything that we see, we focus on the essential information that we need to function successfully.

There is a real penny on the next page so that you can figure out the correct answer to the penny dilemma without actually digging through your purse or emptying out your pocket!

One of the biggest problems that children encounter is encoding failure. How do children know which information is the "right" information to encode? If children are not encoding the relevant information, then how can they utilize that knowledge at a later date? One of our cognitive goals ought to be to help children figure out which information is worthy of our attentional energy and potential encoding.[94]

This is the real penny so that you can figure out the correct answer to the penny dilemma on the previous page without actually getting up to find your purse or emptying out your pocket!

Box 15 The Real Penny [95]

The Architecture of the Mind

When we think of memory, however, it is not usually short-term memory that we are referring to. Information that is stored on a more permanent basis requires what we refer to as "long-term memory." If information in short-term memory is attended to frequently, then it can take up more permanent residence in our memory system. We often refer to the "box model" as a metaphor for the architecture of the mind.[96] It is not that memory is literally stored in boxes but rather that there is a difference between information that we store temporarily and information that we store more permanently.

The Architecture of the Mind

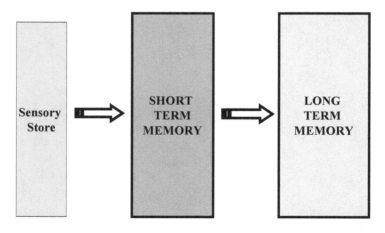

Box 16 The Box Model of Memory[97]

The first box in this model is called the "sensory store." When you focus your attention on something, it enters your sensory store. This is a very brief, temporary store that funnels information into short-term memory. When we look at a book or any visual image, for example, we form an iconic image in our sensory store that is available to us for a fraction of a second before it fades forever. Try the experiment in the box that you'll find on the next page to gain a better understanding of your sensory store and iconic memory. When you're ready, turn the page for a brief second, then close your eyes after 1 second, or a fraction of a second if you can. You will then try to recall what you saw. Remember, do not turn the page until you are ready and don't forget to close your eyes!

In your own time . . . turn the page . . .

Directions: Stare at the letters below for 1 second, then close your eyes and try to remember what you saw.

H	Q	P	L	U
T	M	I	B	A
R	F	Y	Z	W

Box 17 A Test of Your Sensory Store and Iconic Memory

When you closed your eyes, did you see an image of the letters? That is an iconic image. It should have faded after a brief second. While the image is available to you, you should be able to look around it, but once it fades, it should be permanently inaccessible.[98] According to the box model, if information gets to your sensory store and you pay attention to it, then (and only then) can it enter your short-term memory store. If you attend to the information in your short-term memory store, then it may pass into your long-term storage.

Where Is Your Kindergarten Teacher Now?

Now go back to Question #3 at the start of the chapter. Did you remember the name of your kindergarten teacher? This name was stored in your long-term memory, so how were you able to access it almost immediately since (no disrespect intended) you probably didn't attend kindergarten this century? So how did you remember the name? How does our memory work? Where and how is that information stored to allow us immediate access to information that we haven't needed in years? Did you scan through files? Was it like a Rolodex or a Google search?

The truth is that we cannot look into our thought process, or introspect, and figure out how we found that name. Introspection was really the first leap into psychology way back in the 1880s. A German psychologist by the name of Wilhelm Wundt (pronounced "voont" for all our phonics-based readers) played a metronome and asked the participants in his study to describe their immediate conscious experience. This is actually recorded as the first experiment in psychology and the birth of psychology as a field. This type of study was known as "structuralism" and it died a quick death, as people quickly realized that we don't know how we think! We cannot look inside the recesses of our brain and figure out where the information came from.

If you need further proof that introspection doesn't work then read on. Write down your favorite flavor of ice cream in the box below:

My favorite flavor of ice cream is:

Now, how do you know that is your favorite flavor? When I pose this question in my Introduction to Psychology classes, students typically give the following responses:

- I always order that one

- It tastes good

- I don't order any other

- It satisfies me

When probed further with "how do you know that?," in addition to becoming extremely frustrated by the question, they respond:

- My brain tells me

- My taste buds tell me

- My taste receptors respond pleasurably

- Neurons fire in my brain

These responses are interesting and not incorrect, but they don't tap into the inner workings of the brain to reveal the process by which we think about ice cream, or any other cognition. They can't because we can't introspect. We don't know how we think. More than 125 years after Wundt and his metronome, how much do we really know about our own cognitions? We can use CAT scans, PET scans, and MRIs to pinpoint locations in the brain where thinking occurs. We know that language production and comprehension occur in Broca and Wernicke's areas of the brain.[99]

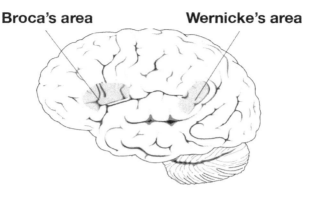

Box 19 Brain Showing the Location of Broca's
Area and Wernicke's Area[100]

We know that vision is processed in the occipital lobe at the back of the brain. We can locate many regions of the brain and pinpoint what they do, and we can follow neural activity around the brain. However, we do not have any direct access to or awareness of the process within our own brain. We cannot introspect and follow a thought today any more than Wundt could a century ago.

Organize Your Thoughts

What we can do is to hypothesize. We can analyze what people remember and forget and we can build a theory. Returning to Question #3, what can we hypothesize about your kindergarten teacher? Cognitive psychology is based on a computer metaphor from the 1950s. We encode information, we store information, and we ultimately retrieve information. At some point, you had to encode your teacher's name. How you encoded it can help to determine how you might have retrieved it. The organizational system in our memory is of paramount importance here.

To understand the memory system, think about 2 neighbors whose garages are side by side. Neighbor A is neat and tidy. This neighbor has tools stored in ascending size order, trays of differently shaped nails, and screws that are labeled and neatly stored—all in all, a meticulously organized garage. Neighbor B, not so much! Neighbor B has too many irons in too many fires. Neighbor B is working on 4 projects simultaneously while starting up a new business and repairing 3 different rooms in his house. Neighbor B has the same tools as Neighbor A but they are randomly thrown about the garage. They have no specific location and just lie in the last place they were used. Now ask yourself this, which neighbor would be better able to locate a specific tool for a specific task, anal-retentive Mr. A or random, slapdash Mr. B?

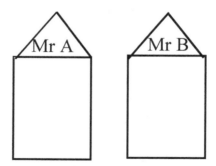

Box 20 Encoding, Storage, and Retrieval in Long-Term Memory

Compare this analogy to your long-term memory storage facility. How you store the information is equally as important as what you store. Bear in mind that long-term memory, unlike STM, has no limit to its capacity (that we know of at least). Also, unlike STM, information does not fall out of long-term memory if it is not attended to! Getting information into long-term storage doesn't seem to be as complex as getting it back out!

Obviously, memory isn't that simple. There are many different types of memories. Maybe your teacher features in a "flashbulb memory." Flashbulb memories are powerful recollections of traumatic events, like where you were or what you were doing when you heard about the death of JFK or the tragedy of 9/11. We think that we remember exactly where we were or what we were doing with amazing detail and clarity, yet recent research suggests that those recollections may not be as accurate as we think.[101]

Perhaps, to encode this teacher's name, you utilized your semantic memory, where you store facts like "all teachers that I've ever had" or states and their capitals. If you enjoyed kindergarten, perhaps you applied the "Pollyanna Principle," whereby pleasant facts that are enjoyable are more easily recalled.[102] Maybe it was easier for you to recall this fact because, unlike Question #1, it was about you. If so, you were demonstrating the "Self-Reference Effect." This effect suggests that it is easier for you to recall information that is about you personally.[103]

Maximizing Memory

Children's long-term memory systems appear to be similar in structure to an adult's memory. It is, once again, the utilization of those memory systems that develops with experience, allowing us to recall more efficiently as we age. Long-term memory can be assessed using recognition or recall paradigms. Children's recognition rates are similar to adult rates.[104] Recognition is essential for multiple choice–style exams that are popular in many schools and national tests. Alternatively, recall rates among children are much poorer than adult rates.

Recall requires children to utilize some type of memory strategy to "retrieve" the information from long-term memory. When children are not successful at recalling information, it could be for a number of strategy-related reasons. Some children do not realize that strategies need to be applied. Some children do not know which strategy to use, and other children fail to use a strategy successfully. Children's memory has been described as passive, non-strategic, and non-planful.[105] Given that these are not the ideal conditions for success, how can we motivate children to be less passive, more strategic, and more planful? Metacognitive research suggests that in our work with children we should use familiar information, familiar situations, make our goal clear, and use a limited set of items. This should allow each child to achieve his or her individual best.

CHAPTER 19

OH, IF I RAN THE SHOW

Crying Out for Change . . .

W e have established that decoding is only a small fraction of the reading process. We have also established that children must:

- Learn to pay attention to what they read
- Visualize the text
- Integrate ideas within a story
- Consider what background knowledge is applicable
- Apply their relevant background knowledge
- Know when to change their perspective when they read

Our reading discussion has culminated in the notion that reading is a dynamic, interactive process that requires the reader to form an ever-changing mental representation of the text. It goes without saying, of course, that children imitate what they see . . .

Let's now establish how we should tackle the teaching component of the reading process. How should we teach children to read within a fun, enjoyable environment where we focus simultaneously on decoding and comprehension skills?

There are 8 key areas that are crying out for change:

1. Reading Levels: The notion of reading levels needs to be redefined so that it aligns with the cognitive capacities of our pre-readers.

2. Proposition Integration: This is a covert process that needs to be made visible to children so that they can learn to build a story into 1 meaningful unit. This is a process that skilled readers do automatically but novice readers need to learn. Storyboards are ideal for this process.

3. Inference-Making Skills: Children need to be taught how to make inferences based on a text. This is a skill that can be practiced and discussed even before the introduction of a storybook or reading practice.

4. Pictures: The use of pictures in books must be addressed since we have definitive research that shows the potential value of this tool that is seriously underutilized. We need to

focus on pictures that represent the text or mirror the action within the story.

5. Background Knowledge: Since the role of background knowledge is so essential to the reading process, we need to find creative ways to incorporate additional information that goes beyond each story. This process should begin before the book is even opened.

6. Sounding Out: We need to focus on teaching the sounds that letters make, not just the names of those letters. We also need to have levels of decoding, starting with phonetically fair words.

7. Environmentally Friendly, Living Books: We need to focus on reading books that encompass the general knowledge of the average pre-reader. We need to integrate the classroom environment into our reading so that children can utilize their existing knowledge to make inferences about the text. If we are able to include their classroom life then children would, quite literally, live their books.

8. Maintaining Parent-Child Reading Time: In any successful reading program, there must be a "read to your child" component. Many parents feel as if they are cheating if their child isn't doing all the "work." Children should not be pressured to read during this parent reading time. Listening skills and comprehension-building strategies develop during this critical interaction. This process is hindered by a parent's

constant focus on asking children to rehearse their decoding skills.

Knowing Which Books to Buy

Each of these 8 areas can be addressed within the concept of "Reading Levels." Look at the myriad of books that are designed to help children read. They often come in a series with "step 1" or "pre-reader" as the introductory book. Pay particular attention to the basic "starter" level books in any one of these collections. They often have small words, short sentences, beautiful pictures, large print, and a limited number of words on the page. These are promoted as the ideal features in books that promote literacy. Now, using your knowledge of the research from previous chapters, think about some of the key aspects of the reading process:

> Small words aren't necessarily the easiest words for children to pronounce.

"The," "try," "once," and "blue" may be short, but they require significant skill to pronounce. Phonetically fair words are far more important than just "small" words. So words like "dog," "up," "over" and "red" are far easier to read because they spell the way that they sound, or are phonetically fair.

Short sentences can often be filled with 2 or more propositions, which make them cognitively taxing.

Simple ideas in short sentences are ideal for novice readers who are focusing a great deal of their cognitive resources on the decoding process. The number of propositions or idea units is far more relevant than the actual length of the sentence.

To compensate for the limited number of words on each page, stories often rely on inferences to fill in the missing information. These inferences often evade the novice reader. Try to find books that contain inferences that resolve themselves within the story or within the child's range of background knowledge. Stories with only 1 or 2 inferences can avoid overcomplicating the reading process.

Pictures enhance comprehension, but only when they actually depict the action or interaction within the text. Make sure your pictures support the interaction within the story and not just the characters or setting within the text.

Multiple pages become overwhelming for novice readers who invariably resort to looking at the pictures or asking an experienced reader to "decode" for them. Try to find books that have a limited number of pages; as an approximate measure, use the child's age as a page guide.

Try Nothing New

A better approach to books for novice readers would be ones that address their cognitive limitations while simultaneously developing their newly emerging comprehension skills. The reading levels described below address these newly emerging skills. They tap into the vast body of research on children's decoding skills, their reading comprehension competence, and their cognitive capabilities. None of these ideas are new; they are just newly compiled into 1 useable format for children.

CHAPTER 20

DISCOVER THE MAGIC: LEVEL 1

Level 1 is designed to introduce children to the concept of text. The goal is to help children to discover the magic of reading.

What's in a Name?

The Title:

Reading begins with the title of the story. Titles are invaluable in the comprehension process. The title allows the readers to access relevant background knowledge that can aid in the understanding of the story by filling in inferred information. The background knowledge accessed through the title can also add to the general enjoyment of the story by allowing readers to predict actions and outcomes based on their own prior experiences. A title can often assist readers in attending to the relevant aspects of the story. All stories and books should begin with the title. The sample book below is called "Sam Fell." Children should discuss the title and anticipate what might happen in the story.

Phonetic Fairness:

Readers ought to know that they should read the title, and it should be a title that they can read with relative ease. To this end, Level 1 uses only phonetically fair words. A phonetically fair word is one that spells the way it sounds or can be "sounded out." "Cat" or "dog" are phonetically fair because they spell the way they sound. Try to sound out the word "cat" by saying the names of the letters "C-A-T." No matter how often you repeat it, it will never sound like the word. Now make the sound that each of these 3 letters makes (not their names, but the sounds): "C-A-T." Now if you blend those sounds together, you can approximate the word "CAT." Phonetically fair words can be sounded out.

In contrast, words that are phonetically unfair cannot be sounded out to enhance decoding. Phonetically unfair words include "the" and "once." They can be mistaken for "readable" words because they are short or appear frequently, but they are deceptively complex because they do not sound as they spell. Even phonetically fair words should be limited in their length. Words should be no longer than 3 or 4 letters in length.

There should only be 3 or 4 words per page and 4 or 5 pages per book. This, along with word length, allows for the short-term memory capacity of the average child. It avoids overstimulation, attentional limitations, and cognitive overload.

Fun

Level 1 should be fun! The books are simple, but they should invite children to discover the magic of reading. To this end, Level 1 books leave something for the child to figure out; that is, they encourage a child to make an inference about the story. In the story below, Sam fell. The story does not say why he fell. The children can, therefore, draw their own conclusions. This type of open-ended inference is essential in reading comprehension. It allows children to be successful at the reading process. The title of the book, "Sam Fell," helps to set the scene. Below, you'll find a sample of the cognitive simplicity of this level:

Sam

Sam ran

Go Sam, go...

No... Sam!

A Picture Paints . . .

Pictures at this Level 1 stage play a key role in defining the quality of the book. A picture should show the action or interaction in the text. At the Level 1 stage, the books are so simplistic in text that the pictures are crucial. Children learn to abstract meaning from the pictures in much the same way that they will go on to extract meaning from the text: They form inferences and they apply their background knowledge to the pictorial representations. These pictures must show the relationship between the components of the story. Comprehension is attenuated when the interactions in a text are the focal point of the illustrations.

Fill In the Blanks

Children can be encouraged to add a page to "Sam Fell" showing why he fell. Their drawing should be preceded by a discussion on running and falling. Perhaps one of Sam's laces was untied or perhaps he tripped. Children can be encouraged to think about the last time they ran or even fell. Utilizing their background knowledge will help them fill in the missing information in the story. This builds their inference-making skills, which are essential for good comprehension. Here the children can invent or design their own inference but, as the reading levels advance, they will have to learn to abstract inferences from both within the text and from their own background knowledge.

Learning Objectives

Level 1 should focus on letting the children build confidence in their ability to read, predict, and comprehend.

There are 10 learning objectives for decoding and comprehension in Level 1:

1. Introduce **prediction skills** that are essential for reading comprehension by encouraging a child to anticipate what might happen, for instance, to Sam as he runs.

2. Explore **elaboration skills** that are essential for reading comprehension by asking children questions such as:

   - "Where do you think Sam is going?"
   - "Why do you think that Sam fell?"

3. **Integrate a child's background knowledge and personal experience** into the story by discussing similar or related experiences in the child's life. This can be shown in pictorial format on a board, the children can verbally exchange ideas, or objects can be collected on a table.

4. **Learn to use pictures** to help make sense of the words on a page.

5. **Develop an understanding of the concept of a title** and its value in the reading process.

6. **Recognize that there is more of a one-to-one correspondence between consonants and their corresponding sounds.**

7. **Develop a child's confidence and fluency in sounding out letters and reading aloud.**

8. **Reinforce the value of pictures and background knowledge** by asking the child to draw (or verbally add) 1 object to the picture that might help the story to make more sense.

9. **Introduce the skill of integrating propositions** as a story is read to the child.

10. **Inference-making skills should be addressed through stories** that are read to the children. For example, we can nurture a child's inference-making skills by asking, "What happened to Sam?" (he fell) followed by, "Why do you think that happened?"

Sounds Like . . .

Level 1 books should work through the following short vowel sounds:

The vowel sounds as heard in:

NOT	MAN	IN
JUST	GET	

Stories could include titles like "Ben's Pen" and "Hot Pot." Remember, all words in this level have to be phonetically fair.

Sample Phonetically Fair Words That Spell As They Sound

cat	sat	mat
big	pig	wig
pit	sit	fit
dog	log	fog
run	fun	bun
red	bed	fed

Word length can be increased during the latter stages of this level, once the basic words have been mastered. Word length can be increased provided that it does not interfere with phonetic integrity. Words like "banana," "trip," and "sister" may be longer but they can still be sounded out by a novice reader.

Double Trouble

Once these basic words have been mastered, Level 1 should continue with the introduction of double vowels. These books should use "ee" and "oo" but the stories should still be phonetically fair. Titles could include "Feet" and "Cook Book."

Vowel families can be introduced during this level. These should be enjoyed in a colorful and fun environment with simple drawings to help with recognition. The words should, however, still maintain phonetical fairness. Remember to sound out the letters to emphasize the similarities. Also remember that sounding out means using the sound that the letter makes, not the name of the letter. An example of a vowel family is given below:

Welcome to the ood family!

food

wood

good

mood

hood

The "ood" word family is designed to enhance decoding skills.

The sounds of the words in the English language ought to come alive for our novice readers. Set up an "ee" box or an "oo" box and let the children collect words that belong in each box.

Practice, familiarity, and experience will help to increase their fluency, and a fun, lively environment will help to sustain their interest.

Blend

When these concepts have been mastered, blended consonant sounds should be introduced which, in keeping with Level 1, should be phonetically fair. Blended consonants include, but are not restricted to, the list below:

SH

TH

CH

WH

QU

A Proposition for You

All Level 1 books can be characterized by their propositional content. Each book has 1 proposition or idea unit per page. We need to actively teach children to integrate those propositions. That is a Level 1 skill. Children need to hold 1 proposition, or idea unit, in working memory while simultaneously learning a new idea or proposition. This is called proposition integration. To actively teach proposition integration, this covert, internalized process must be externalized. The storyboard is an ideal tool for this process. Each proposition in the story is added to the board so that children can, essentially, build a story.

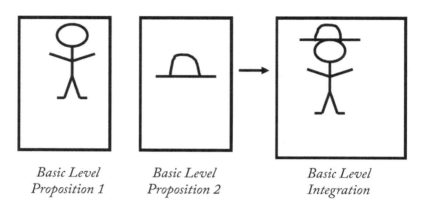

Basic Level   *Basic Level*   *Basic Level*
Proposition 1   *Proposition 2*   *Integration*

Each Component of the Story (or proposition) Is Placed on the Storyboard to Build a Complete Story (and Integrate Propositions)

Clearly this is not designed to be an exhilarating book but rather a stage in the reading process. In this basic level of proposition building, children sound out "boy" and then take the boy and place him on the storyboard. They repeat this process with "h-a-t," hat. When they reach the third page, they can put the hat on the boy (on the storyboard). This may seem like a pedantic task to adults, but that is because it has become such an automated skill for competent "comprehenders." Adults are no longer aware of the complexities of proposition integration because they have automated this process. Again, we are taking a covert, automated process and externalizing it for the purpose of reading comprehension. The skills of proposition assembly and proposition integration are essential in the reading comprehension process. Storyboards are ideal for this task because they isolate 1 concept in the comprehension process and help children focus on the task at hand. This activity, proposition integration, will become internalized as it develops into a more automated process. Obviously, the above example is extremely simplistic. Proposition integration can be, and often is, an extremely complex process. As this skill develops, children can work on increasingly more complex propositions in higher reading levels. The goal, once again, is for readers to develop competence using these essential comprehension tools. It is only by building these solid foundations that readers will have the skills to sustain them as comprehension becomes more demanding and increasingly complex in a social studies chapter or a Shakespearean sonnet.

Write Your Own . . .

Level 1 also includes bookmaking. Staple 2 or 3 pages together and create a book with children. The goal here is for your child to experience the success of creating a book. There are a multitude of ways to accomplish this task, and the method should be determined by the child. Children could cut pictures from magazines, draw pictures, or dictate the story to be written by an adult. Remember to allow time for your child to read the story to you, and remember to praise the process as well as the product. Digital cameras are great for homemade books. Act out a very simple story by taking 4 or 5 photos. Print 1 picture out for each page, then add 1 or 2 words to each page. This allows children to bring their own knowledge of the photo to the story. It is an ideal way to build reading comprehension skills because the child knows so much more than just the picture or the words on the page.

Book Particulars

To summarize, Level 1 books are characterized by:

- A title page
- Phonetically friendly, short words (34 letters)
- 3 to 5 pages per book
- Pictures that match the actions in the story
- 1 proposition or idea unit per page (or sentence)
- An open-ended inference

Slow and Steady

Level 1 should not be rushed. It is not important when a child learns to decode, per se. Rather, it is important that children explore all of the skills that are required for competent reading comprehension. Remember the failure rates presented in the literature and how sixth or eighth grade compared with third or fourth grade? Why is there a decline in our children's reading performance as a function of grade level? The answer lies in the cognitive demands of the task: As the necessity to comprehend texts becomes more demanding, mastery of these Level 1 skills becomes more imperative. How often have you read an entire page of text but, by the end of the page, you can't actually recall what you read? This is a proposition integration issue, as well as a need to focus attention on the task at hand. Similarly, how often have you read a set of instructions but not actually been able to visualize what is being asked of you? The ability to visualize a text is crucial in reading comprehension, but it is a skill that must be learned. Both proposition integration and visualization skills take attentional energy. Coupled with inference-making skills, they form the foundations of comprehension, just as letter sounds form the foundation of decoding.

Read It Aloud

Reading aloud to children is imperative at this stage. Children should discuss the stories that are being read to them. They should talk about the characters and get to know them. They should discuss the location or setting of the story and they should discuss the action or plot. Children should be encouraged to anticipate what might happen next. They should be encouraged to think about the effect of changing one or more aspects of the story. Each of these activities serves as a precursor for comprehension of the written text. All too often our pre-readers are focused on the decoding of print, and these vital skills go underdeveloped.

Active Listening

By listening, since they are freed from the cognitive demands of decoding, their attention should be focused on the visualization process that underlies proposition integration. There are many different techniques that could be used to accomplish this goal. During listening comprehension, readers could close their eyes and picture or visualize the story, or children could build storyboards to keep pace with the story. The use of puppets is also ideal. Acting out these simple stories is also a great way to focus on meaning and textual inferences.

When we read aloud to children, we should try to make our voices as animated as possible. Different characters can have different voices, and the mood of the story can be portrayed by a shift in the voice. We can encourage our children to use or make simple costumes, like a pillowcase for a cape. We can plan ahead and find an object or two to accompany our story, like sitting on a plastic egg while reading about Horton the elephant (he hatches an egg!) in *Horton Hears a Who*. Acting out scenes in a story is an ideal way to bring the text to life for our pre-readers. Our goal is to invite our children into the story to explore with us.

Test-Free Assessment

Assessing comprehension levels during this shared reading experience is important. Questioning children about the inferences within the text is an ideal way to measure levels of understanding. Asking questions that involve rote memorization will not tap into comprehension skills.

A Problem Shared:

Teacher and parental encouragement are essential at this early level of literacy. For a child, it can be difficult to maintain the motivation to invest time and energy in a process that has such a delayed outcome. The value of children hearing a story and sharing that quality time with a teacher and parent really needs to be emphasized. We need to separate book time into 2 different concepts: a time for "listening" and a time for our child to practice decoding and reading to us. We need to reinforce the positive value of telling our child the pronunciation of a difficult word. Again, that isn't "cheating." It promotes enjoyment in the shared reading process, alleviates pressure on the child to "get it right," and helps in our quest to develop lifelong readers.

Similarly, there is a delicate balance that needs to be struck between asking questions to promote literacy and "interrupting" a child's story with too many questions or superfluous facts. Children provide great feedback; watch their faces and body language, and they'll tell you.

Make Time

It is important to find time in their (and our!) overscheduled lives to keep reading to your children. It is also important to take time to enjoy the process of reading with our children. It is vital that our goal at storytime is not to get to the end of the story so that we can continue with the daily routine of baths or dinner or bed. We should vary the time of day that we read to our children. If we always read at bedtime, then our children might begin to negatively associate reading with bedtime.

Measuring Failure

Level 1 really begins at birth when we tell our neonates stories and read them simple books. Children can explore the basic components of reading for many years. Our educational system has put a premium on one single aspect of this stage (decoding), giving the impression that 5-, 4-, or even 3-year-olds can be proficient readers. If we look at all of the skills that are actually required in developing the comprehension process, then we should upwardly expand that age range. Earlier is not better. We have no current system in our existing educational practices to measure the success of proposition integration, visual representation, or inference-making skills. Currently, we measure failure rates.

Discovering the Magic of Reading

One Level 1 goal ought to be to help children discover the magic of reading so that they spontaneously choose to read. Reading should be part of the child-initiated, child-directed script of pre-schoolers.

During Level 1, we should mention the sounds that letters make whenever it comes up in conversation, but the majority of our day ought to be spent nurturing comprehension skills and a love for reading.

CHAPTER 21

BUILDING SOLID FOUNDATIONS: LEVEL 2

Level 2 expands on Level 1 skills. Inference building can now be more pictorially directed. In the "Sam Fell" story, for example, a rock can be depicted to the left of Sam. This would suggest to the mature reader that Sam tripped over the rock. The picture below shows the pictorial simplicity of Level 2 books. Once again, the focus is on illustrating the interaction within the text or highlighting the inference using a pictorial clue.

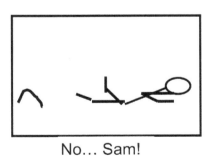

No... Sam!

Embedded Inference in Pictorial Representation

What Can You Infer?

Children need to learn to look for those inferences. In Level 2, we can insert them into the pictorial representations; we'll call them "embedded inferences." Children need to be taught to look for these embedded inferences. During the cognitive delay between automating decoding skills and learning to comprehend the printed word, pictures serve as the ideal medium for developing inference building skills. In other words, most children can "decode" pictures.

By Level 3, inferences should be incorporated into the text. A Level 3 reader ought to have the available cognitive resources to extract inferences from the textual clues. At Level 2, however, the concept of inferences is still being developed. There is a shift from the open-ended inferences in Level 1 to the embedded inferences in Level 2, but they are still primarily contained within the pictorial representations to promote comprehension success.

A Wizard for the Day

Decoding is also expanded by addressing the 5:18 problem; that is, 5 vowel letters making 18 different vowel sounds.

To encourage decoding skills, children in Level 2 can now learn about the "magic e." Each child can become a wizard for the day and transform vowels using the "magic e" rule: When a word ends with the letter "e," the vowel in the middle of the word is pronounced using the name of that vowel rather than a sound. The box below is filled with examples of words that have a "magic e" on the end, causing the vowel to be sounded out using its own name.

Magic E

date	hole	tide
gate	sale	hide
mate	tale	rate
pole	male	late
mole	ride	fate

These Words All Conform to the Magic E Rule

Children can begin by taking words that exist in the English language as 3-letter words, then they can add the "magic e" and watch them transform.

mat → mate

hat → hate

fat → fate

3-Letter Word Transformations Using the Magic E Rule

Silly Words

The concept of the "idiot word" can be modified and renamed to account for words that don't spell the way they sound. These words should be displayed on a "silly wall" so that children can appreciate the fun and variety in our language. Displaying these words in the classroom or the home will enhance sight word recognition without the dreaded use of flash cards. These words can be written or they can be cut from magazines, newspapers, or food cartons. Whenever possible, a drawing or visual prompt should accompany these words to enhance recall.

Examples of "silly words" are listed below:

Words That Don't Spell As They Sound—"Silly Words"

the	sky	knife
choice	wrote	floor
knee	these	risky
door	cheese	brought

Examples of "silly words" formally known as "idiot words"

Silly Families

Many of these phonetically unfriendly, or "silly words," have word families so they are particularly fun to make word families with. Highlighting the word endings in the same color allows children to reinforce their auditory processing with visual stimulation. A sample chart of the "ight" family is below:

Welcome to the ight family!

The "ight" word family designed to enhance sight word recognition

Picture This

Level 2 should continue to focus on pictorial representations that accompany the printed word. All of the pictures should follow the content of the text and actually portray the action in the stories. These pictures allow a child to visualize the text. They serve as a visual demonstration of how individual propositions integrate within a story. They can also be used as an excellent tool to begin the inference process.

As letter sounds are becoming more easily identified or automated at this level, more cognitive capacity is available to focus on proposition integration and inference building.

There are 9 learning objectives in Level 2:

1. Success in integrating an increasing number of propositions per story.

2. The continued development of inference-making skills so that children can find clues within the story to make inferences beyond the text. Level 2 should see a shift from open-ended inferences to pictorially embedded inference comprehension.

3. The integration of background knowledge into the story so that children can comprehend as they read. This background knowledge should come from the child's immediate environment.

4. Less reliance on storyboards as the processes of proposition building and proposition integration become internalized.

5. The continued development of combining letter sounds to form words.

6. Increased recognition of phonetically unfriendly words that do not spell the way that they sound.

7. Recognition of phonetically unfriendly word families.

8. Increased recognition of blended sounds including but not limited to "wh," "th," "sh," and "ch."

9. Fluency in changing the consonant letters in a vowel family to create and recognize new words.

CHAPTER 22

SHIFTING FOCUS: LEVEL 3

In Level 3, there is a shift from a focus on pictorial representations to a strong textual emphasis. This shift should occur not as a function of age, per se, but rather as a function of cognitive readiness. There will be an obvious move away from the laborious sounding out of words to an ease of recognition and automaticity in decoding skills. This ought to allow more attention to be paid to comprehension skills, such as inference-making and the application of background knowledge.

What Can You Infer?

This shift to automaticity in decoding will allow for a further change in the focus of reading materials. Pictorial inference-making skills will be replaced by textual inferences. There will be an overall decrease in the number and complexity of pictures within a book. This will encourage readers to internalize the process of proposition integration. Readers at this level will develop fluency in building the idea units of a story internally and making the necessary inferences accordingly.

Inferences at Level 3 should be textually based. These should begin as open-ended inferences so that readers can fill in their own ideas.

Example of an open-ended inference: Tired Jim

Jim was very tired. It was only 6 in the evening, but he couldn't stop yawning. He put on his pajamas as quickly as he could. Jim quickly brushed his teeth and crawled into his bed. As Jim lay in bed, he thought about his long, tiring day.

Open-ended inference: Why was Jim tired?

As this skill becomes more accomplished, texts should contain embedded inferences so that the reader can find the stated reason for an inference within a text.

Example of an embedded inference: Tired Jim

Jim was very tired. It had been a long day. Jim thought about his day. He had played 7 amazing soccer games. His team had won every game. He quickly put on his pajamas and crawled into his bed. As he lay in bed, Jim thought about his wonderfully exciting day.

Embedded inference: Why was Jim tired?

Propositions Galore!

Level 3 will also show a marked increase in propositional use within 1 sentence. Whereas Levels 1 & 2 restricted the use of propositions to 1 per sentence, Level 3 does not make this distinction. Sentences can increase in propositional count, and therefore in complexity, as the reader's skill level develops.

It's All in Your Head

The internalization of these comprehension skills is the defining characteristic of the Level 3 reader. In order to build propositions and make inferences from a text, the Level 3 reader will need to be able to apply background knowledge where necessary. As a result, Level 3 books should still focus on themes and concepts within the reader's area of knowledge. This creates less of a cognitive strain and allows for optimal development and success in comprehension.

Familiarity

Ideal Level 3 books should focus on a child's daily routine, school, home life, hobbies, and family. Since these reading levels do not correspond to any specific age, it becomes increasingly difficult to generalize about ideal texts for Level 3 children. A trip to any bookstore or library will confirm that, although it is time-consuming and labor-intensive, Level 3 readers can be accommodated by finding books that relate to a child's daily routine, interests, and hobbies. There are a large variety of books on similar topics written at different reading levels.

Level 3 (General) Learning Objectives:

Once again, our goal in Level 3 books is to find material that has moved beyond a strong pictorial content.

- Text should now move beyond 1 or 2 propositions per sentence to allow for more complex proposition integration.
- There should be inferences throughout the story to develop inference-making skills. These inferences can be open-ended or textually embedded.
- Background knowledge, however, should still be within the experiential range of the reader.

Phonetically Fluent

Level 3 focuses on fluency in phonetically unfair words. The 5:18 vowel letter to sound ratio is addressed at this level. Rhyming word families help children to develop familiarity with these complex issues.

Welcome to the OU family!

cloud	proud	loud
doubt	tout	grout
trout	about	sound

double trouble is not in our family!

Level 3 Development of Phonetically Unfair Words

There are many vowel families that need to be addressed. 5 are listed below. They involve recognition, which develops as a result of exposure. Making families and focusing on a sound for the week helps with familiarity.

Phonetically Unfriendly Vowels

OU OI OA EA AI

Phonetically Unfriendly Vowels

Unstable Consonants

Level 3 also addresses phonetically unfair consonants like the "ph" sound. Consonants are usually more stable; as a result, we can refer to consonants that change their sound as "unstable consonants." These unstable consonants include ph and gh.

when ph = f

elephant	telephone	phase
phantom	phrase	prophet

Unstable Consonant Family

There are also silent consonants to contend with like silent "k" and silent "h." They belong in the unstable consonant family also.

Silent K	**Silent H**
knife	ghost
know	when
knot	honor
knee	rhyme
knight	white

Silent Consonants in the Unstable Consonant Family

These complex sounds should not be introduced at the expense of proposition integration or inference building. They should not be so overwhelming that incorporating background knowledge takes a proverbial "back seat" to decoding. They should be introduced gradually so that readers maintain their confidence. Books at this level should contain many of these word families to encourage recognition and success.

Long-Range Inferences

Level 3 readers should, by the end of this level, be able to make textually embedded inferences that are designed to have part of the inference at the beginning of the story and the other vital information at some point later in the text. These "long-range" inferences necessitate that the reader builds a mental representation of the text and maintains it in working memory throughout the passage. This is an advanced skill that takes time to develop.

Tom's Surprise

Tom ran home. He climbed the narrow steps to his front door.

He threw his backpack on the top step by his front door.

He ran inside his home to find his sister Jill. Jill was in her bedroom.

Tom told his sister the good news.

Jill followed Tom down to the front door.

Tom ran outside to show Jill his surprise.

As Jill ran outside she tripped over something and fell.

Poor Jill.

Sample of a Long-Range Textually Embedded Inference

The text does not explicitly state that Jill tripped over the backpack. She may not have tripped over the backpack at all. There could be any number of explanations why Jill tripped. However, a plausible explanation, based on the content of the story, would be that she tripped over her brother's backpack that he had thrown on the top step. Asking readers to suggest why Jill tripped provides access into their mental representation of the text. If the reader has built a solid depiction of the facts, then the backpack would be a good response. If the reader is processing the information and adding background knowledge to the text, then a past experience, like tripping over the family cat, would be a plausible explanation even if the text did not mention a family cat sitting on the step. This would be an excellent response to an open-ended inference. This text, however, does provide a clue, and by the completion of Level 3, skilled readers ought to be able to identify the textually embedded clue in this inference.

Learning Objectives

The 10 learning objectives in Level 3 are:

1. Emphasis on a shift from strong pictorial reliance to the textual domain as decoding skills strengthen.

2. Automated decoding of phonetically fair words.

3. Identification of open-ended inferences.

4. Identification of textually embedded inferences.

5. Identification of long-range textually embedded inferences. Remember, long-range, textually embedded inferences have partial information located throughout the text.

6. Application of background knowledge to a text to interpret inferences.

7. Success at integrating multiple propositions within a sentence.

8. Success at building mental representations from text-based stories.

9. Recognition of phonetically unfair vowels and consonants through repeated rhyming games and repetition.

10. Increase in reading fluency with modified texts that focus on phonetically unfair families.

CHAPTER 23

SKILLS THAT LAST A LIFETIME: LEVEL 4

By Level 4, decoding ought to be fluent. Readers ought to be adept at making textual inferences, both open-ended and embedded. They ought to be accomplished at making long-range inferences. Building a story through proposition integration ought to be a well-rehearsed skill and background knowledge should be routinely incorporated into the text whenever required.

Level 4 learning objectives are:

1. Proficiency in decoding and sight word recognition

2. Proficiency in proposition building and integration

3. Proficiency in mental representation of any text

4. Proficiency in inference making: open-ended, embedded, and long-range

5. Proficiency in applying background knowledge to a text

6. Proficiency in extracting new information from a text

Meaningful Reading

Levels 1, 2, & 3 treat reading and comprehension skills as an END GOAL. They are concerned with the process of learning to extract meaning from print. Level 4 moves beyond teaching decoding and comprehension to focus on using the reading process as a means to an end. The Level 4 stage accentuates reading for meaning with a purpose. Reading, by Level 4, has become a vehicle through which new facts and information can be learned. Competent comprehension skills alleviate many of the risk factors associated with poor reading performance. Level 4 readers can use the reading process to study world history or learn about the anatomy of a fly. They can use their solid comprehension skills to read texts that go beyond their personal background knowledge. They can now actually use new texts to expand their background knowledge.

Although purposeful reading is a Level 4 goal, giving reading a purpose was also a Level 1 goal. Purposeful reading is actually synonymous with focusing on comprehension skills. Since less skilled readers lack the cognitive capacity to decode and comprehend, this process is emulated for them so that they can approximate the end goal before they are cognitively ready. It is essential to practice reading for meaning throughout the reading process so that these skills continue to develop.

Since the great majority of our young children can't yet decode with competence, the 4 levels of this reading program utilize a variety of techniques that modify texts to accommodate children's cognitive availabilities. Emerging readers can focus on the meaning of a text by using pictures and simplified texts to practice these skills and accomplish the goal of successful comprehension. By Level 4, our readers should have the requisite experience to comprehend independently.

Level 4 readers should be able to make mental representations of a text. They should be able to integrate complex propositions and make inferences. This should result in their ability to extract meaning from a textual passage. Level 4 readers can apply their background knowledge to a story. They can also increase their background knowledge by reading new information.

CHAPTER 24

PUT THE FUN BACK INTO READING!

Any reading program, including the 4-level reading program that is outlined in the previous chapters, relies heavily on a child's desire to learn to read. Our communal goal, therefore, must be to create a "need to read" for our perspective readers.

The need to read and the need to write should be interconnected.

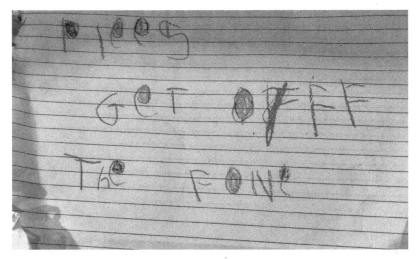

A self-explanatory note from one of my children . . .

They are both based on the essential need of all human beings to communicate:

Our basic need to communicate
("Please ask Finn if you want some of this
chocolate or there will be an issue"!)

Let's do this in our kindergarten, pre-kindergarten, and child care classrooms (as many already do). Let's put some fun back into learning!

Children learn by doing and they learn through play. Encourage your children to incorporate reading and writing into their play.

Remember, we may not always know what they are writing . . . but they do!

This was a story that clearly made sense to this pre-reader! (I also have no idea what it says!!)

Let's set up a grocery store, a post office, and a bank within the classroom and in our homes for our preschoolers and kindergarteners. Let's use the dress-up corner and the kitchen area to play "house" and "shop." Let's give the children roles and let them play. Send 1 to the bank, send 1 to the store, and send 1 to write and mail a letter! These are activities that require reading and writing, so let's utilize them!

OO the Fun!

We can also play with our children to encourage their early literacy. Making "oo" words turned out to be a delicious activity:

First we wrote them . . . then we ate them!!

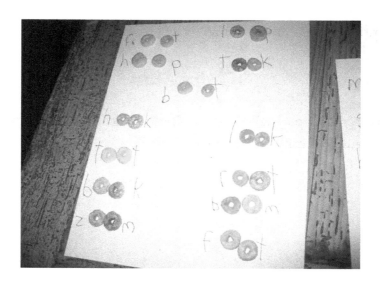

The Grocery Store

Give Reading a Purpose

In both our homes and our classrooms, we should have child-run stores—what better way to give reading a purpose! Children can plan meals for the kitchen area. They can use picture/word cards to help them compile a shopping list. They can then visit the store and buy the items on their "list." This game has enormous learning potential. You can focus on all vegetables one week or you can include sorting tasks, like separating the fruit from the vegetables. You can use only words that spell the way they sound so that the children can think about sounding them out. Words like "bun," "corn," "nuts," or "hot dog" all spell the way they sound. The pictures ensure that this is a self-correcting task.

Each Food Item in the Supermarket Would Have a Matching Card

As a child's comfort level increases, the foods' degree of difficulty can be changed. Foods that spell the way they sound but are slightly longer, such as "butter," "pasta," and "water," can be added. The third level of foods ought to include blended sounds including "fish" or "chips." The final class of words, always accompanied by pictures, ought to include words that bear little or no correlation to their spelling. Foods like "soup," "peas," or "tofu" could be included in this category.

Paying 1 penny for each food item would be a fun math activity. As the semester progresses, the food prices could be raised; for example, to 2 pennies per item.

Sorting the food back onto the appropriate shelves at the end of the activity is also an excellent opportunity for lessons in categorization and nutrition.

The Post Office

Each classroom should have a mailbox, and each child should take turns delivering the "mail." If each piece of mail is properly labeled with the child's name, then the children will quickly learn who's who. Let the children wear name tags in the classroom to help with word recognition and turn this game into a self-correcting activity. Mail can include notes that are to be sent home to parents or letters from classmates. It can also be a fun way to organize art projects that are sent home!

The post office could also sell stamps for 1 penny each. This will encourage children to count. They could develop this idea and increase postage to 2 pennies later in the year.

The supermarket and the post office help to create a more relaxed, risk-free environment that takes the pressures of learning off children. This way, they can have fun and learn through their play.

Play at Reading

There are plenty of games that have already been developed and packaged that also create this risk-free learning environment for children to learn though their play. Games like Zingo encourage children to have fun playing bingo while simultaneously being exposed to pictures and their corresponding printed text.

Excellent Games Are Available to Promote a Risk-Free Learning Environment [106]

Of course, Level 1 & 2 readers would benefit far more from phonetically friendly bingo that you could, ostensibly, make yourself.

  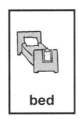

bug **car** **bed**

Make Your Own Bingo Word Game with Phonetically Friendly Words

Underlying Skills

Reading may be the linchpin of children's future learning, but it is certainly not the only skill that demands our attention. Planning and remembering play a key role in cognitive development. In our society, we put a premium on extra-curricular activities, and they certainly do have their place in child development. We should not, however, underestimate the value of more mundane acts such as chores, responsibilities, and free time.

The planning and organizing that is involved in each of these activities is the same planning and organizing that we need in reading comprehension success and in all of our children's academic endeavors. For example, when children help to sort laundry, initially it may not seem like an academic activity, but it has many of the components that we strive to master in kindergarten. We can sort clothes according to size. We can organize them according to color. We can match socks, which, as you know, can become quite intricate as we try to discern one similar pattern from another. These activities—sorting, organizing, and matching—are essential cognitive milestones. Our children can master these while they help us maintain our homes—what could be better?

The responsibilities of setting the table, loading the dishwasher, or sweeping the floor teach a child self-worth. Children take pride in contributing to a family, and this effort should be nurtured. It teaches children the importance of working together and the value of a shared family experience. Children as young as 2 or 3 years old can help to set the table.

Teenagers, as long as they live under your roof, can also help. Family chores teach children to follow through to completion. They can show children the value of 1 small act within a complex series of actions. They also nurture independence and foster industriousness.

Free time can help a child develop time management skills and creativity. Free time can also develop a child's emerging sense of self, while also supporting their independence. When children run between too many scheduled activities, they sometimes become dependent on an adult to organize them, plan for them, and manage their time. Free time gives children breathing space. It allows them to reflect, contemplate, and grow. Great plans can be made during free time, and children need time to invent and create. They need time to be spontaneous. They need time to decide what they like to do and what they wish they'd done instead. A great deal of planning and organizing can evolve from having no set agenda.

Another way to focus on planning and remembering is through children's games. Simple card games like Memory are ideal to encourage children to develop their recall skills. As long as we make sure that we set out the appropriate number of cards for the maturity level of our child, this can be a great cognitive tool for recall skills. As you play, watch and see what type of strategies your child is utilizing during the game. Some children keep staring at the card that they are trying to remember. Others try to line the cards up or move them slightly. Verbal rehearsal is a common strategy, along with visual clues like "it's behind the blue one." It is the act of developing a strategy and trying to utilize it that is so valuable in this situation. Adults can also model good planning and remembering strategies for their children, although there is a fine line between modeling and formally instructing. Each child develops his or her own systems for recall and the superficial gains from imposing adult ideas on a child are short lived.

Memory Games Foster Planning, Remembering, and Organization [107]

Make double sets of your photographs from family trips or events and use these to make your own Memory game. If you decide to make a game out of index cards, make sure that words are supported by pictures for a positive learning experience and that the level of detail is appropriate for the age of the child.

Other fun games that develop strategy use are Connect 4, chess, backgammon, and checkers. Think of the cognitive challenges that are posed: planning ahead, problem solving, anticipating a move, thinking, and remembering.

Strategy Promoting Games like Connect 4,
Chess, Checkers, and Backgammon

No Microwave Beep or Gas Gauge

Children don't beep like a microwave when they are ready to learn! They also don't signal the amount that they have learned like your car's gas gauge measures your gas level! We should focus on the opportunities we can create for our children rather than looking for that elusive outcome. We should focus on the process of learning, instead of the final product.

What Does Learning Actually Look Like?

Let's be honest, would we even recognize learning if we saw it? Does exploration have a form? Children construct knowledge from the world around them. If we provide the ideal tools, we need only leave the construction up to our children.

Reading and Learning Should Be Fun!

Conclusion: It's Time . . .

It's time to reinvent reading. Now that you know there is so much more to reading than decoding, it's time . . .

It's time to refocus your attention on the age-appropriate tasks that children can engage in as they develop a sense of literacy. Chapters 1 through 15 have shown you the component processes that are involved in this complex task.

As reading is the linchpin of all future learning, we have an obligation to make sure that we are doing right by our children. Chapters 18 through 23 detail a blueprint for reading from birth through literacy that you can adapt to fit your home, classroom, or your curriculum.

The whole language approach to learning is an ideal paradigm. Incorporating reading into everyday life will nurture children's natural curiosity and capitalize on their internal motivation to learn. Chapter 24 combines life experiences with the reading process for an integrated approach to learning.

It's time . . .

A FINAL NOTE

THIS MAY BE LESS DIFFICULT TO READ

Certainly no one ever said that parenting was easy! No one ever said that teaching was easy, either. When parents try to teach, it can become a doubly frustrating experience . . .

I hope that this book has shed some light on some of the difficulties that children experience as they navigate a path that has become second nature for us. Remember, they are not like us. Their brains are wired differently. They think differently. They process information differently. If you want to succeed, learn to think as they think. Learn to process information as they process information.

As I say "goodbye" to my last child and wave him off to begin his university experience, I urge you to remember that it's a journey that takes 18 long years. If you fixate on the outcome, the payoff, the final product, then it will be a bittersweet moment when you say your "goodbyes." Try, instead, to enjoy the journey, the mistakes, the learning curves, and those "precious moments." Let your children lead, and learn to follow . . .

Good luck, and enjoy each moment of your journey.

ENDNOTES

1. https://www.shutterstock.com/image-vector/red-rose-isolated-on-white-vector-1205470477

2. Logan, G. D. (2004). Attention, automaticity, and executive control. In A. F. Healy (Ed.), *Experimental cognitive psychology and its applications*. (pp. 129-139). Washington, D.C.: American Psychological Association Press

3. Roese NJ, Vohs KD. (2012). Hindsight bias. *Perspect Psychol Sci.*, 7(5):411–426. doi:10.1177/1745691612454303

4. Sweet, R. W. (1996). The century of miseducation of American teachers. The National Right to Read Foundation. Retrieved March, 19, 2005

5. New York State School Board, 2005. NAEP Nation's Report Card, 2019.

6. August, D.L, Flavell, J. H. & Clift, R. (1984). Comparison of comprehension monitoring of skilled and less skilled readers. *Reading Research Quarterly*, 20, 39–53

7. Paris, S.G., Wasik, B.A. & Turner, J.C. (1996). The development of strategic readers. *Handbook of Reading Research, 2*, 609–640.

8. https://www.greatschools.org/gk/articles/high-achiever-remedial-college/

9. https://nces.ed.gov/programs/coe/indicator/cnb/reading-performance

10. https://wowwritingworkshop.com/about-1-in-5-students-need-remedial-help-in-college/

11. https://www.npr.org/sections/ed/2016/04/06/472970364/taking-high-school-courses-in-college-costs-students-and-families-nearly-1-5-bil

12. https://allaccess.collegeboard.org/affordability-and-to-days-middle-income-families

13. Alberini, C. M., & Travaglia, A. (2017). Infantile Amnesia: A Critical Period of Learning to Learn and Remember. *The Journal of neuroscience, 37*(24), 5783–5795. https://doi.org/10.1523/JNEUROSCI.0324-17.2017

14. Johnson, M.K., & Raye, C.L. (1998). False memories and confabulation. *Trends in Cognitive Sciences, 2*, 137-145

15. http://upload.wikimedia.org/wikipedia/commons/2/2e/Gray739-emphasizing-hippocampus.png

16. Nickerson, R. S. (1998). Confirmation Bias: A Ubiquitous Phenomenon in Many Guises. *Review of General Psychology, 2*(2), 175–220. https://doi.org/10.1037/1089-2680.2.2.175.

17. Leapfrog Books. http://fatwallet.cachefly.net/i/deals/leapfrog-tag-reader-books-online-coupon.jpg

18. Look and Learn ABC's. http://www.orange32.com/design/wp-content/uploads/2007/06/abc_cover.jpg

19. Jumpstart PreK. http://www.miescuelita.org/new/images/jumpstart.jpg

20. https://www.shutterstock.com/image-photo/penny-macro-both-sides-one-american-19823449

21. https://yourbabycanlearn.com

22. Goldwert, L. (2012). Your Baby Can Read Settles False Advertising Claim. https://www.nydailynews.com/life-style/baby-read-settles-false-advertising-claims-ftc-article-1.1147276

23. Reader Rabbit. http://www.musiccataloger.com/images/
    READER%20RABBIT%20PLAYTIME%20FOR%20
    BABY%20&%20TODDLER%20-%20SOFTWARE_
    LG.jpg

24. http://www.geniusbabies.com/babywow.html

25. https://the-true-baby-einstein.fandom.com/wiki/Baby_Mo-
    zart?file=Baby_Mozart_%25281998%2529_VHS.png

26. Carstens, C. B., Huskins, E., & Hounshell, G. W. (1995).
    Listening to Mozart may not enhance performance on
    the revised Minnesota Paper Form Board Test. *Psycho-
    logical Reports*, 77(1), 111–114. https://doi.org/10.2466/
    pr0.1995.77.1.111

27. Rauscher, F. H., & Shaw, G. L. (1998). Key Components of the
    Mozart Effect. *Perceptual and Motor Skills, 86*(3), 835–841.
    https://doi.org/10.2466/pms.1998.86.3.835

28. Steele, K. M., Bass, K. E., & Crook, M. D. (1999). The mystery
    of the Mozart effect: Failure to replicate. *Psychological
    Science, 10*(4), 366–369. https://doi.org/10.1111/1467-
    9280.00169

29. https://www.shutterstock.com/image-vector/illustration-ba-
    by-crazy-about-tv-1930928264

30. Bangerter A, Heath C. (2004). The Mozart effect: tracking
    the evolution of a scientific legend. *Br J Soc Psychol., 43*(Pt
    4):605–623. doi: 10.1348/0144666042565353

31. https://www.shutterstock.com/image-vector/cute-ein-
    stein-210904495

32. https://encrypted-tbn1.gstatic.com/images?q=tbn:ANd-
    9GcTGS12wLrKJnfKgq2q8VCAX1OwMUvm-
    RQKHsqyZg9m4b9H2AFAyW

33. https://i0.wp.com/sitn.hms.harvard.edu/wp-content/
    uploads/2015/02/brain-512758_640-copy.png

34. https://neurosciencenews.com/files/2014/10/neuron-diagram. jpg

35. https://encrypted-tbn2.gstatic.com/images?q=tbn:ANd-9GcQvdFsML7oXIxMFQHERy_X5hyXZJxk7otMe-pq3V-ProawD7SNi6

36. Huttenlocher PR, Dabholkar AS (1997) Regional differences in synaptogenesis in human cerebral cortex. *J Comp Neurol 387*: 167-178.

37. Greenough, W. T., & Black, J. E. (1992). Induction of brain structure by experience: Substrates for cognitive development. In M. R. Gunnar & C. A. Nelson (Eds.), *Developmental behavioral neuroscience* (pp. 155–200). Lawrence Erlbaum Associates, Inc.

38. Feinberg, I. (May 1, 2017). *Why is synaptic pruning important for the developing brain?* Scientific American. https://www.scientificamerican.com/article/why-is-synaptic-pruning-important-for-the-developing-brain/

39. Piaget (1896-1980)

40. Gibson, Eleanor J., and Harry Levin. 1975. *The psychology of reading.* Cambridge, MA: MIT Press

41. William James. "Great Men, Great Thoughts and the Environment." *Atlantic Monthly 46* (1880): 441-459.

42. https://commons.wikimedia.org/wiki/File:William_James,_philosopher.jpg

43. Chall, J. S. (1979). The great debate: Ten years later, with a modest proposal for reading stages. In L. B. Resnick and P. A. Weaver (Eds.), *Theory and Practice of Early Reading.* Hillsdale, NJ: Earlbaum

44. Chall, J. S. (1979). The great debate: Ten years later, with a modest proposal for reading stages. In L. B. Resnick and P. A. Weaver (Eds.), *Theory and Practice of Early Reading.* Hillsdale, NJ: Earlbaum

45. Markman, E. M., & Gorin, L. (1981). Children's ability to adjust their standards for evaluating comprehension. Journal of Educational Psychology, 73(3), 320–325. https://psycnet.apa.org/doi/10.1037/0022-0663.73.3.320.

46. Markman, E. M. (1977). Realizing you don't understand: A preliminary investigation. *Child Development, 48*, 986–972; Markman, E. M. (1979). Realizing that you don't understand: Elementary school children's awareness of inconsistencies. *Child Development, 48*, 996–972

47. Markman, E. M. (1979). Realizing that you don't understand: Elementary school children's awareness of inconsistencies. *Child Development, 48*, 996–972

48. Markman, E. M., & Gorin, L. (1981). Children's ability to adjust their standards for evaluating comprehension. *Journal of Educational Psychology, 73*(3), 320–325. https://doi.org/10.1037/0022-0663.73.3.320.

49. Rubman, C.N. & Waters, H.S. (2000). A, B, Seeing: The role of constructive processes in children's comprehension monitoring. *Journal of Educational Psychology, 92*(3), 503–514

50. Harris, P. L., Kruithof, A., Terwogt, M. M., Visser, T. (1981). Children's detection and awareness of textual anomaly. *Journal of Experimental Child Psychology, 31*, 212-230 https://doi.org/10.1016/0022-0965(81)90013-8

51. Paris, S., Newman, E. (2009) In book: *Handbook of Research on Reading Comprehension* (pp.32–53) New York: Lawrence Erlbaum Associates

52. Perfetti, C.A. (1985). *Reading Ability*. New York: Oxford University Press

53. Perfetti, C.A. (1985). *Reading Ability*. New York: Oxford University Press

54. https://publicdomainvectors.org/en/free-clipart/Vector-illustration-of-vintage-red-car/30817.html

55. Geisel, T. (1960). *Green eggs and ham*. New York: Beginner Books

56. https://commons.wikimedia.org/w/index.php?search=dollars&title=Special:MediaSearch&go=Go&type=image

57. Piaget, J. (1954). The Construction of Reality in the Child. New York: Basic Books. https://psycnet.apa.org/PsycBOOKS/toc/11168

58. https://www.shutterstock.com/image-vector/cartoon-baby-holding-blanket-181179728

59. Piaget, J. (1954). The Construction of Reality in the Child. New York: Basic Books. https://psycnet.apa.org/PsycBOOKS/toc/11168

60. Piaget, Jean. (1952). *The origins of intelligence in children*. New York: International Universities Press.

61. Bransford, J. D. & Johnson, M.K. (1972). Contextual prerequisites for understanding: Some investigations of comprehension and recall. *Journal of Verbal Learning and Verbal Behavior, 11*, 717–726

62. Bransford, J. D. & Johnson, M.K. (1972). Contextual prerequisites for understanding: Some investigations of comprehension and recall. *Journal of Verbal Learning and Verbal Behavior, 11*, 717–726

63. Bransford, J. D. & Johnson, M.K. (1972). Contextual prerequisites for understanding: Some investigations of comprehension and recall. *Journal of Verbal Learning and Verbal Behavior, 11*, 717–726

64. Rubman. C., Schultz, S., Murphy, R. & Zevallos A. (2003) The Development of Inference Making Skills In Pre-School Children. Society for Research in Child Development. Tampa, Florida

65. Piaget, Jean. (1952). *The origins of intelligence in children*. New York: International Universities Press

66. Piaget, Jean. (1952). *The origins of intelligence in children*. New York: International Universities Press

67. McClelland, J. L., & Rumelhart, D. E. (1981). An interactive activation model of context effects in letter perception: I. An account of basic findings. *Psychological review, 88*(5), 375.

68. Nelson, Katherine & Fivush, Robyn & Hudson, Judith & Lucariello, J.. (1983). Scripts and the development of memory. Contributions to Human Development, 9, 52–70. 10.1159/000407966

69. Anderson, S.J., & Conway, M.A. (1993). Investigating the structure of autobiographical memories. *Journal of Experimental Psychology: Learning, Memory and Cognition, 19*, 1178-1196.

70. Pichert, J. & Anderson, R.C. (1977). Taking different perspectives on a story. *Journal of Educational Psychology, 69*, 309–315

71. Shakespeare (1597)

72. Charlotte Bronte (1847)

73. Rubman, C.N. & Waters, H.S. (2000). A, B, Seeing: The role of constructive processes in children's comprehension monitoring. *Journal of Educational Psychology, 92*(3), 503–514

74. Gambrell, L.B. & Bales, J. R. (1986). Mental imagery and the comprehension-monitoring performance of fourth and fifth grade poor readers. *Reading Research Quarterly, 21*, 454–464; August, D.L, Flavell, J. H. & Clift, R. (1984). Comparison of comprehension monitoring of skilled and less skilled readers. *Reading Research Quarterly, 20*, 39–53; Shriberg, L.K., Levin, J., McCormick, C. C. & Pressley, M (1982). Learning about "famous" people via the key word method. *Journal of Educational Psychology, 74*, 238–247

75. Garner, R. (1981). Monitoring of passage inconsistency among poor comprehenders: A preliminary test of the "piecemeal processing" explanation. *The Journal of Educational Research, 74*(3), 159–162. https://doi.org/10.1080/00220671.1981.1 0885302

76. Brown, A. L., Bransford, J.D., Ferrara, R. A. & Campione, J.C. (1983). Learning, remembering and Understanding. In P. H. Mussen (Eds.), *Handbook of child psychology. Vol.3. Cognitive development*, New York: Wiley

77. Rubman, C.N. & Waters, H.S. (2000). A, B, Seeing: The role of constructive processes in children's comprehension monitoring. *Journal of Educational Psychology, 92*(3), 503–514

78. Jimenez, L. (2018) How to Reform Remedial Education https://www.americanprogress.org/article/remedial-education/

79. Bush, G (2001). No Child Left Behind Act (NCLB) https://georgewbush-whitehouse.archives.gov/news/reports/no-child-left-behind.html

80. Bush, G (2001). No Child Left Behind Act (NCLB) https://georgewbush-whitehouse.archives.gov/news/reports/no-child-left-behind.html

81. "Reading and Mathematics Scores Decline during COVID-19 Pandemic," Nation's Report Card.gov, accessed October 9, 2022, https://www.nationsreportcard.gov/highlights/ltt/2022/

82. Katie Lobosco, "Education Secretary Miguel Cardona Says 'Kids Can't Suffer Anymore' after Tumultuous Year," CNN. com, February 9, 2022, https://www.cnn.com/2022/02/09/politics/education-secretary-miguel-cardona/index.html

83. https://www.act.org/content/act/en/research/services-and-resources/data-and-visualization/grad-class-database-2022.html

84. https://leadershipblog.act.org/2022/10/GradClassRelease2022.html

85. Tulving, E., & Psotka, J. (1971). Retroactive inhibition in free recall: Inaccessibility of information available in the memory store. *Journal of Experimental Psychology, 87*(1), 1–8. https://doi.org/10.1037/h0030185

86. Miller, G. A. (1956). The magical number seven, plus or minus two: Some limits on our capacity for processing information. *Psychological Review, 63*(2), 81–97. https://doi.org/10.1037/h0043158

87. https://pixabay.com/photos/magic-black-magic-hat-wand-1469121/

88. Atkinson, R. C. & Shiffrin, R. M. (1968). Human Memory: A proposed system and its control processes. In K. W. Spence and J. T. Spence (Eds.), *The psychology of learning and motivation: Advances in research and theory (Vol. 2)*, pp. 89–105. New York: Academic Press

89. Craik, F.I.M. & Lockhart, R.S. (1972). Levels of processing: A framework for memory research. *Journal of Verbal Learning and Verbal Behavior, 11*, 671–684

90. https://www.shutterstock.com/image-vector/young-girl-thinking-about-something-trying-144653330

91. Brown, A. L., Bransford, J.D., Ferrara, R. A. & Campione, J.C. (1983). Learning, remembering and Understanding. In P. H. Mussen (Eds.), *Handbook of child psychology. Vol. 3. Cognitive development*, New York: Wiley; Baddeley, A.D. (1996). *Working memory.* Oxford, UK: Oxford University Press; Hitch, G.J. & Towse, J. N. (1995). Working memory: What develop? In F.E. Weinert & W. Schneider (Eds), *Memory performance and competencies: Issues in growth and development.* Mahwah, NJ: Erlbaum; Zelazo, P.D., Frye, D. & Rapus, T. (1996). An age-related dissociation between knowing rules and using them. *Cognitive Development, 11*, 37–63

92. Nickerson, Raymond & Adams, Marilyn & Beranek, Bolt. (1979). Long-Term Memory for a Common Object. *Cognitive Psychology, Vol. II*, 287-307.

93. Nickerson, Raymond & Adams, Marilyn & Beranek, Bolt. (1979). Long-term memory for a common object. *Cognitive Psychology, 11*, 287–307. 10.1016/0010-0285(79)90013-6

94. Siegler, R.S. & Alibali, M. A. (2005). *Children's Thinking*. Prentice Hall, Upper Saddle River, NJ

95. https://www.shutterstock.com/image-photo/penny-macro-both-sides-one-american-19823449

96. Atkinson, R. C. & Shiffrin, R. M. (1968). Human Memory: A proposed system and its control processes. In K. W. Spence and J. T. Spence (Eds.), *The psychology of learning and motivation: Advances in research and theory (Vol. 2)*, pp. 89–105. New York: Academic Press

97. Atkinson, R. C. & Shiffrin, R. M. (1968). Human Memory: A proposed system and its control processes. In K. W. Spence and J. T. Spence (Eds.), *The psychology of learning and motivation: Advances in research and theory (Vol. 2)*, pp. 89–105. New York: Academic Press

98. Sperling, G. (1960). The information available in brief visual presentation. *Psychological Monographs, 74*(11), 1–29

99. Broca, P. (1861). Remarques sur le siege fe la faculte du langage articule, suivies d'une observation d'aphemie (perte de la parole). *Bulletin de la Societe Anatomique (Paris) 36*, 330–357; Wernicke, C. *Der Aphasische Symptomenkomplex* (Breslau, Poland: Cohn & Weigert, 1874

100. https://study.com/cimages/multimages/16/brocaw-er6291537793825950576.jpg

101. Neisser, U. & Harsch, N. (1992). Phantom flashbulbs: False recollections of hearing the news about *Challenger*. In E. Winograd & U. Neiwwer (Eds.) *Affect and accuracy in recall: Studies of "flashbulb memories."* Cambridge University Press

102. Matlin, M. W. (2004). Pollyanna Principle. In R. Pohl (Ed.), *Cognitive illusions: Handbook on fallacies and biases in thinking, judgment and memory.* Hove, England: Psychology Press

103. Rogers, T. B., Kuiper, N. A., & Kirker, W. S. (1977). Self-reference and the encoding of personal information. *Journal of Personality and Social Psychology, 35*(9), 677–688. https://doi.org/10.1037/0022-3514.35.9.677

104. Flavell, J. H., Green, F.L. & Flavell, E.R. Development of children's awareness of their own thoughts. *Journal of Cognition and Development, 1*, 97–112

105. Brown, A. L., Bransford, J.D., Ferrara, R. A. & Campione, J.C. (1983). Learning, remembering and Understanding. In P. H. Mussen (Eds.), *Handbook of child psychology. Vol. 3. Cognitive development*, New York: Wiley

106. https://www.shutterstock.com/image-photo/children-hands-touching-white-cards-letters-1204900864

107. https://www.shutterstock.com/image-vector/little-boy-girl-play-memory-board-2149522141

108. https://www.shutterstock.com/image-vector/illustra-tion-baby-crazy-about-tv-1930928264

DISCUSSION QUESTIONS

1. Go back to the "Facts and Myths" at the start of the book—why do you think that some people struggle with these concepts? Think about "sounding out" words, classical music, small versus bigger words & readability, looking at pictures, reading to your child . . .

2. When you were a child, who read "to" you, and "with" you?

3. What was your favorite book as a child? Do you remember why it was your favorite?

4. As a child, which aspects of the reading process did you struggle with? If you have children or if you teach children, do they struggle to understand the printed word?

5. Why do you think that so many people ascribe to the "earlier is better" philosophy with reading and early childhood education? Why is this not necessarily the best approach to reading and early childhood education?

6. Why do you think that 1 in 5 college students need remedial reading help in their freshman year?

7. Now that you have read this book, what did you learn about the developing brain and how we process information? What was new to you? What surprised you? Think about the hippocampus, the myelination process, the reticular formation, vision, proposition integration, schematic knowledge, societal pressure, and reading comprehension success . . .

8. Now that you have read about many of the components that are involved in the reading process, what would you do differently if you were helping a child to learn to read? Think about background knowledge, pictures, titles, decoding, inferences, perspective-taking, book choice, and promoting successful reading comprehension . . .

9. How do schools promote a "love for reading"? What could they do to encourage even more children to love reading?

10. Was this book "difficult to read"? Explain why or why not . . .

CPSIA information can be obtained
at www.ICGtesting.com
Printed in the USA
JSHW012123161122
33318JS00005B/28